The Fight for *Sola Scriptura*

# The Fight for *Sola Scriptura*

*Reclaiming the Exclusive Authority of Scripture in the Modern Age*

Matthew Cserhati

WIPF & STOCK · Eugene, Oregon

THE FIGHT FOR *SOLA SCRIPTURA*
Reclaiming the Exclusive Authority of Scripture in the Modern Age

Copyright © 2025 Matthew Cserhati. All rights reserved. Except for brief quotations in critical publications or reviews, no part of this book may be reproduced in any manner without prior written permission from the publisher. Write: Permissions, Wipf and Stock Publishers, 199 W. 8th Ave., Suite 3, Eugene, OR 97401.

Wipf & Stock
An Imprint of Wipf and Stock Publishers
199 W. 8th Ave., Suite 3
Eugene, OR 97401

www.wipfandstock.com

PAPERBACK ISBN: 979-8-3852-3090-7
HARDCOVER ISBN: 979-8-3852-3091-4
EBOOK ISBN: 979-8-3852-3092-1

VERSION NUMBER 01/13/25

Figure 5, "The Descent of the Modernists," originally published in *Seven Questions in Dispute* by William Jennings Bryan (New York: Revell, 1924). Taken from https://commons.wikimedia.org/wiki/File:Descent_of_the_Modernists,_E._J._Pace,_Christian_Cartoons,_1922.jpg.

Emphases added to Scripture quotations.

Unless otherwise stated, Scripture quotations are from the New King James Version, copyright @ 1982 by Thomas Nelson, Inc. Used by permission. All rights reserved.

Scripture quotations marked WSE are from the Westminster Study Edition of the Holy Bible, copyright @ 1948 by Westminster. Used by permission. All rights reserved.

The author would like to thank Tim Lewis for personal discussions that helped in the writing of the section on open theism.

For I testify unto every man that heareth the words of the prophecy of this book, if any man shall add unto these things, God shall add unto him the plagues that are written in this book: And if any man shall take away from the words of the book of this prophecy, God shall take away his part out of the book of life, and out of the holy city, and from the things which are written in this book.

Rev 22:18–19

# Contents

The Status of *Sola Scriptura* Today | 1
The Nature of God's Word | 5
The Historical Development of *Sola Scriptura* | 8
What Is *Sola Scriptura*? | 17
Extra-Biblical Revelation: The Charismatic Movement | 36
The Erosive Tide of Liberalism | 76
Roman Catholicism: Man Supplements God's Word | 94
Refutation of Roman Catholic Arguments against *Sola Scriptura* | 108
Comparison of Major Ideological Currents That Deny *Sola Scriptura* | 117
Eastern Orthodoxy: A Mix of Mysticism | 120
Dispensationalism: Cutting the Scriptures in Half | 126
Evangelical Errors Concerning *Sola Scriptura* | 135
Conclusion | 147

*Bibliography* | 149
*Subject Index* | 155
*Scripture Index* | 171

# The Status of *Sola Scriptura* Today

Introduction

THE ROMAN CATHOLIC CHURCH wants to debunk it. To the charismatic movement it is unknown. The liberals try to get around it, and erode it bit by bit. This is the way that many today are trying to undo the biblical teaching of *sola Scriptura* so that they can introduce their own man-made ideas into their version of Christianity.

In this modern day and age of ours, the Bible is held in disrepute and even contempt by many. In a post-Darwinian era, the Bible is looked upon as nothing more than just a mere collection of fables and fairy tales, the stuff of legend and make-believe. Hardly anyone can seriously repeat the words of Ps 119:97: "O how love I thy law! It is my meditation all the day." The Bible is the object of scorn, hatred, and rejection. Many people reason that if evolution, masquerading as a monolithic theory of origins, has disproven the account of creation in Genesis, then the Bible could possibly be incorrect in other parts as well, such as the life and person of Jesus and salvation.

As such, and since the Bible has been increasingly removed from the public sphere, especially from public schools, the Bible is not being taught anymore, therefore the Bible is less and less known, to the point of utter ignorance in many cases, even within the church. It can be said that *sola Scriptura* has almost become a lost teaching.

I can well remember a conversation that I had with the head pastor of a medium-sized charismatic church, who had been at his position for at least twelve years. He looked to be over fifty, at least. I asked him what he understood the term *sola Scriptura* to mean. He fumbled for words, and it was quite odd to see that the man had not even heard of the term.

In later years it turned out that this very same church gave its political support for Joseph Biden, supported LGBTQ ideology, and supported the Biden vaccine mandate. If you deny *sola Scriptura*, you will unavoidably become liberal in your theology. Then, you will also become liberal in your morals as well. The charismatic movement, the Roman Catholic Church, and liberal theology are all related in a similar way.

In the politically correct milieu of the modern age, we are saturated with the ideas of pluralism, relativism, and multiculturalism. The Bible is treated as just one book among many. The exclusive secular use of rationalism has led many to think that there is no absolute truth and, furthermore, that truth cannot even be determined.

For example, the philosopher René Descartes claimed that the only thing one can know for certain is that one thinks.[1] This is the ultimate end of methodological doubt. This is because only God's word can claim to be absolute truth, because it is given by an omniscient, all-knowing God. If people reject God, they also reject all chances of knowing absolute truth.[2] This has paved the way to irrationalism, which has made inroads into the church as well. This happens once the mind of man becomes the ultimate arbiter of truth, repeating the age-old sin of Adam and Eve in the garden of Eden when they rejected God's word and ate from the tree of the knowledge of good and evil.

Some believe that one cannot arrive at the true meaning of the Bible by using grammatical analysis and reasoning, illuminated by the Holy Spirit.[3] This opens people's minds to mysticism and the mythologization and allegorizing of the Bible. In other words, people can make the Bible mean whatever they want it to mean. All faiths are equal and true, leading to false ecumenism and the toleration of sects. No one faith can be declared right over any other faith.

The church has reacted to this phenomenon in several ways. One of the ways the church has reacted is by jettisoning bits and pieces of the Bible, here and there, thus slowly and surely eroding the word of God until we have nothing left. This is the way of liberalism. Orthodox teachings such as creation, the fall into sin, the flood, miracles, the virgin birth, the

---

1. Descartes, *Discourse on the Method*.
2. Pratt, *Every Thought Captive*, 23–32.
3. Crampton, *By Scripture Alone*, 247–49.

resurrection have all been abandoned in some form or another in the liberal churches. Liberals do this to appease Bible critics and atheists. This has even led to some liberal pastors openly becoming atheists.

A curious example of jettisoning parts of the Bible by splitting it up into different sections that are valid in different time periods and among different peoples is characteristic of the theological trend called *dispensationalism*, which merits its own discussion as a class of theology opposed to *tota Scriptura*, a teaching derived from *sola Scriptura*.

Another way the church has responded to the threat of naturalism is to deemphasize the rational and logical aspect of the Christian faith, and to overemphasize the emotional aspects and to hyper-spiritualize religion. This is the path that the charismatic movement has taken. Besides deemphasizing the Bible, the charismatic movement also overemphasizes a whole slew of extra-biblical forms of what it views as valid forms of divine revelation (tongues, visions, prophecies, etc.), thereby also removing emphasis from the Bible. Whereas liberalism emphasizes smaller and smaller portions of the Bible, the charismatic movement removes emphasis from the Bible and places it elsewhere, such as human emotion and experience.

Third, it would be beneath some people in the church to jettison any part of the Bible; however, they would be willing to reinterpret the Bible in the face of external pressure due to extra-biblical authorities. Such is the case with theistic evolution, which buckles and bows before evolutionary theory, masquerading as a proven scientific teaching. In this case the unwitting theistic evolutionist interprets the account of Genesis not in the light of other parts of the Bible, but rather on current, trendy scientific theories. This is eisegesis and not exegesis.

Fourth, since the teachings of various cults is contrary to and outside of the Bible, the cults must reinforce belief in their false teachings with false authorities that they set up parallel or even over and against the Bible. Thus, these groups are also opposed to *sola Scriptura* with all their vigor.

Such example denominations are the Roman Catholic Church, the Eastern Orthodox Church, and the Adventist Church. Some churches also add their own books besides the Bible, such as the Book of Mormon. Other groups, such as Jehovah's Witnesses, claim that they define what is true biblical teaching, claiming a canon above a canon. This they do to strengthen the teaching authority of their own church. Some of these groups pick and choose which parts of the Bible suit them best, such as the cafeteria Catholics.

Another way that the denial of the principle of *sola Scriptura* affects the church is in worship. Since the Bible is the sole highest authority in all questions, it also informs us of how we conduct worship, which is a practical aspect of our faith. False worship is displeasing towards God, since we are attempting to worship him on our own terms, with our own ideas. In this way we are not worshipping God, but our own idol. The way God is to be worshipped is set down in the Bible very well, and not following what the Bible says about worshipping God aright amounts to a practical denial of *sola Scriptura*.

The Bible exhorts the church to watch out for grievous wolves who shall enter the church to destroy the flock (Acts 20:29). The state of the church has become so grievous today that false prophets are openly tolerated. This is what is epitomized in the biblical figure of Jezebel, who seduces God's servants to commit spiritual fornication (Rev 2:20). This sad state is due to the rejection of the teaching of *sola Scriptura*. The multiplication of the different myriads of denominations today, each contradicting one another, is also a result of the rejection of *sola Scriptura*. This is easily understood, since if the authority of the Bible is rejected, anyone can introduce their own false teaching as an authority alternative to the Bible.

# The Nature of God's Word

> The words that I speak unto you, they are spirit, and they are life.
> JOHN 6:63

## Introduction

BEFORE WE EVEN BEGIN talking about *sola Scriptura*, let us take some time to examine some of the qualities and the character of God's word in the Bible. This is because the Bible is a unique book compared to all other books in all human history.

God uses the Bible to communicate to us. As opposed to pictures and images, the Bible gives us precise information. God exerts his lordship via his speech. God's presence, control, and authority are all made manifest by his word. God is a speaking God, and God is present and among us, and is not silent. He is not a distant God, like the God of the deists. This is all because God wishes to have a living relationship with us as his creatures. That is why we are not to reverence images, but rather to call upon the name of the Lord as a form of communicating with God. When God speaks, he is heard; only unregenerate unbelievers feign not to hear God's voice because they try to suppress it within themselves (Rom 1:18).

The Word of God is also *Trinitarian* in nature. Jesus Christ is the Word of God (John 1:1–3). The Word emanates from God the Father, through Christ, and by the Holy Spirit. All three persons of the Trinity take part in this divine knowledge because all three Persons are one God.

Jesus Christ says that "the words that I speak unto you, they are spirit, and they are life" (John 6:63). God's words are living words. They are living because they are true. They accomplish what God intended them to do.

God's word never returns to him void. Ps 19:7–8 says, "The law of the Lord is perfect, *converting the soul*: the testimony of the Lord is sure, *making wise the simple*. The statutes of the Lord are right, *rejoicing the heart*: the commandment of the Lord is pure, *enlightening the eyes*."

Psalm 29 gives us a description of the power of God's word. This is described in vv. 3–9: "The voice of the Lord is upon the waters: the God of glory *thundereth*: the Lord is upon many waters. The voice of the Lord *is powerful*; the voice of the Lord is *full of majesty*. The voice of the Lord *breaketh the cedars*; yea, the Lord breaketh the cedars of Lebanon. He *maketh them also to skip like a calf*; Lebanon and Sirion like a young unicorn. The voice of the Lord *divideth the flames of fire*. The voice of the Lord *shaketh the wilderness*; the Lord shaketh the wilderness of Kadesh. The voice of the Lord *maketh the hinds to calve*, and discovereth the forests: and in his temple doth every one speak of his glory."[1]

Notice all the words that describe action in these verses: thunders, brakes, makes them skip, divides flames of fire, shakes the wilderness. These words describe the action, power, and majesty of God's word. God truly is there and directs the course of history by his word. God acts in his creation as well. Through divine concurrence God acts through his laws actively, and not passively, like a mechanical engineer winding up one of his machines who then lets it go to work on its own. God acts by, with, and through the laws of nature that he has created. God does this every day from sunrise to sunset: "The mighty God, even the Lord, hath spoken, and called the earth from the rising of the sun unto the going down thereof" (Ps 50:1).

God expresses his will in his word. And of course, his will is the law since God does not wish us to break his law and thereby sin against him. These three are one, they are not separate from one another. These three— God's word, his will, and his law—are all unified in Jesus Christ, who is the word of God. God gave his law to the Jewish people at Mount Sinai. These are the Ten Commandments, which serve as headers to the rest of the law, of which there are 613 in the Old Testament.

When God made a covenant with his people, he proclaimed blessings to them if they kept his word, and curses if they broke it. In later periods the role of the prophets was to apply God's law to the situation that

---

1. The unicorn may denote the rhinoceros, but it may even mean an extinct species of horse with horns. This is not impossible—narwhals are a whale species with horns. Other mammals, including reindeer, have large ornamental horns on their heads.

the people were in, and to remind them of God's displeasure when they sinned. In this sense the prophets weren't imparting any new information to the people; rather they were reminding the people of God's law, which he had revealed to them earlier.

This is the so-called *ministerial* usage of God's word, when pastors, teachers, or exegetes simply interpret what is in God's word. The *magisterial* usage of God's word is when additions are made to it, like how Congress enacts new laws. The latter is practiced by false churches that deny *sola Scriptura*, most prominently the Roman Catholic Church.

### Inerrancy and the Incarnation

God's word is sufficient for us. God has the power to communicate his will to us. Jesus Christ, the Son of God, is the Word in flesh. Furthermore, Jesus is inseparable from his revelation. Cults and false philosophies tend to separate Christ from the word of God, but by doing so, they create a false Christ for themselves, so they can uphold their own presuppositions (2 Tim 4:3).

Jesus parallels the word of God in several ways. Just as Jesus Christ is both God and man in one person, so the Bible is also God's word for us, written by fallible men, in one book, yet without error. God can reveal his infallible, inerrant word using sinful, fallible men. To use a metaphor, God can draw a straight line using a crooked stick! Jesus Christ was both God and man, and even though he underwent all temptations that we do, yet he was without sin. Similarly, though the Bible was written by fallible men, God can preserve his word from all error.[2]

This is important to note, since several philosophies that have a false hermeneutic also have a low view of God's word. Since God's word is inseparable from God himself, therefore these false philosophies also have a differing view of God himself! As such, the authority of Scripture will also suffer.

---

2. Geisler and Roach, *Defending Inerrancy*, 306–9.

# The Historical Development of *Sola Scriptura*

> Then the brethren immediately sent Paul and Silas away by night to Berea. When they arrived, they went into the synagogue of the Jews. These were more fair-minded than those in Thessalonica, in that they received the word with all readiness, and searched the Scriptures daily to find out whether these things were so.
> ACTS 17:10–11

### *Sola Scriptura* Was Taught by the Early Church

IN ORDER TO UNDERSTAND the concept of how authority was understood in the early church, we have to see how Scripture relates to tradition. This will help us understand how the early church viewed what is known as the principle of *sola Scriptura*.

First, Paul writes to the Thessalonians in 2 Thess 2:15: "Therefore, brethren, stand fast, and hold the *traditions* which ye have been taught, whether by word, or our epistle." Paul later writes in Gal 1:6–8: "I marvel that ye are so soon removed from him that called you into the grace of Christ unto another gospel: Which is not another; but there be some that trouble you, and would pervert the gospel of Christ. But though we, or an angel from heaven, preach any other gospel unto you than that which we have preached unto you, let him be accursed."

Later, the apostles summarized their teaching into a piece of literature called the Didache, which is Greek for "teaching." The Apostles' Creed is also a highly condensed summary of the Christian faith.

We should not be afraid of the word "tradition." Tradition in Greek is παράδοσις (*paradosis*), which means something that is passed on. In our churches today, we share the gospel with nonbelievers. In effect, we are passing on the "tradition" of the gospel. This is because the content of tradition in the early church exactly overlapped or was superimposed on the information content of the Scriptures. There was no difference. The key is that it was the same information content, one written down in Scripture, and the other handed down in oral format.[1] This means that the apostolic teaching is uniform. It has one *source*, not two. It can be transmitted in written, scriptural format and orally. Thus, there are two *modes* of transmission from one single *source* of information.

This is described in 1 Cor 15:1–4: "Moreover, brethren, I declare to you the gospel which I preached to you, which also you received and in which you stand, by which also you are saved, if you hold fast that word which I preached to you—unless you believed in vain. *For I delivered to you* first of all that which I also received: that Christ died for our sins according to the Scriptures, and that He was buried, and that He rose again the third day according to the Scriptures."

Here Paul is handing down the same gospel that he received from others, the tradition, or παράδοσις (*paradosis*). This tradition is "a dynamic of handing over and receiving or a living and active transmission of the church's preaching."[2] The gospel is that Christ died for our sins. Yet where does Paul receive the gospel? As it was revealed to the believers in the *Scriptures. Two* modes of transmission but only *one* source. The early church held that the true faith was contained in the church's continuing teaching tradition, which overlapped with the Scriptures.[3] The early Christians held the gospels to be the memoirs of the apostles, a written form of the sermons that they preached orally.[4]

An early Christian document called the Didache, compiled before the end of the third century, which is allegedly the teaching of the twelve apostles, also speaks about the authority of the Scriptures: "Now concerning the apostles and prophets, deal with them as follows in accordance with the rule of the gospel."[5]

---

1. Mathison, *Shape of Sola Scriptura*, 19–21.
2. Williams, *Evangelicals and Tradition*, 6.
3. Kelly, *Early Christian Doctrines*, 30.
4. Kelly, *Early Christian Doctrines*, 33, 39.
5. Holmes, *Apostolic Fathers*, 155.

Polycarp (AD 69–155), a disciple of the apostle John and bishop of Smyrna, held that the ultimate authorities were Jesus Christ, together with the apostles, who authored the gospels, as well as the prophets of the Old Testament. He makes no mention of extra-biblical revelation.[6]

Irenaeus (ca. AD 130–200) opposed any kind of secret apostolic traditions, available to only a few inducted into gnostic mysteries. Rather, he appealed to the public tradition of the church. The written form of the apostolic proclamation constituted the cornerstone and foundation of the faith.

Clement of Alexandria (ca. AD 150–ca. 215), who also fought against Gnosticism, stated, "But those who are ready to toil in the most excellent pursuits, will not desist from the search after truth, till they get the demonstration from the Scriptures themselves."[7]

Along with Irenaeus, Tertullian (ca. AD 155–220) didn't make any contrast between Scripture and tradition but claimed that the oral preaching of the apostles was written down in Scripture. What is also important about Tertullian's thinking was that he rejected "the idea that the Apostles 'did not reveal to all men' but instead 'proclaimed some openly and to all the world, whilst they disclosed others (only) in secret and to a few.'"[8] To him, the Scriptures furnished the rule of faith.[9] Tertullian also espoused the idea that Scripture is enough for the church to decide truth. He made it a point that if one needs to go beyond Scripture, then that is a sign of unbelief.

In his book *Against the Heresy of One Noetus*, Hippolytus (ca. AD 170–236) described the Holy Scriptures as the unique standard of the knowledge of God.

Cyprian, bishop of Carthage (ca. AD 200–258), writes in a letter against bishop Stephen on baptism: "Let nothing be innovated, says he, nothing maintained, except what has been handed down. Whence is this tradition? Whether does it descend from the authority of the Lord and of the Gospel, or does it come from the commands and the epistles of the apostles? For that those things which are written must be done, God witnesses and admonishes, saying to Joshua the son of Nun: 'The book of this law shall not depart out of thy mouth; but thou shalt meditate in it day

---

6. Kelly, *Early Christian Doctrines*, 31.
7. Mathison, *Shape of Sola Scriptura*, 25–26.
8. Mathison, *Shape of Sola Scriptura*, 25.
9. The rule of faith is that body of knowledge or truth that everything is measured by. The rule of faith judges all things, and nothing judges the rule of faith.

and night, that thou mayest observe to do according to all that is written therein'" (Josh 1:8). He also writes, "Nor ought custom, which had crept in among some, to prevent the truth from prevailing and conquering; for custom without truth is the antiquity of error."[10]

As we can see from Cyprian's writings, he understood what he called *custom* to be a body of statements that were foreign to the apostolic teachings. These customs were innovations made by men, which were added to the apostolic deposit of faith.

After Cyprian, the great theologian Athanasius (AD 296–373) said that Holy Scripture is the apostolic tradition, and there is no other source of tradition. Athanasius said, "The sacred and inspired Scriptures are sufficient to declare the truth," and "Divine Scripture is sufficient above all things."[11]

John Chrysostom (AD 349–407) held that the Bible was the sum of all necessary knowledge, and that everything in it was clear. Vincent of Lérins (d. ca. AD 450) believed that the Scriptures were more than sufficient for all purposes.[12]

The great theologian Augustine (AD 354–430) also placed the Scriptures above all other sources of authority. In his work *On the Catechising of the Uninstructed*, he writes: "But if it happens that his answer is to the effect that he has met with some divine warning, or with some divine terror, prompting him to become a Christian, this opens up the way most satisfactorily for a commencement to our discourse, by suggesting the greatness of God's interest in us. His thoughts, however, ought certainly to be turned away from this line of things, whether miracles or dreams, and directed to the more solid path and surer oracles of the Scriptures."[13] In another work, *On the Good of Widowhood*, Augustine asserts the primacy of Scripture: "For holy Scripture setteth a rule to our teaching, that we dare not 'be wise more than it behoveth to be wise,'" with reference to Rom 12.[14]

## *Sola Scriptura* in the Middle Ages

During the Middle Ages, starting from the eleventh to the fifteenth century, several heretical and semi-orthodox groups were formed in opposition

10. Mathison, *Shape of Sola Scriptura*, 28.
11. Mathison, *Shape of Sola Scriptura*, 30.
12. Kelly, *Early Christian Doctrines*, 42–43.
13. Augustine, *Catechising of the Uninstructed*, 3:288–89.
14. Augustine, *Good of Widowhood*, 3:442.

to the Roman Catholic Church. These groups were formed as a response to the excesses and the secularism and worldliness of Rome. For example, several mendicant groups, such as the Poor of Lyons, were formed as a response to the luxuries and avarice of the clergy.

These groups also formulated their own doctrines and denounced doctrines of the Roman Catholic Church that they deemed heretical and erroneous. For example, Henry the Monk (?–1148), who was originally a priest who became a monk, was a wandering preacher who preached against the Roman Catholic teaching on the Eucharist. He claimed that administering the sacraments should not be done without evangelical support (i.e., from the Gospels). He is quoted as saying, "I accept the Scriptures of the New Testament, by which I verify and corroborate the aforesaid statements." He also accepted the writings of Augustine of Hippo and other early theologians but did not give them final authority.[15]

Henry the Monk was an early appeal to the authority of Scripture as opposed to the teachings of the church. After him, Valdes of Lyons (ca. 1140–ca. 1205), otherwise known as Waldes, Valdesius, Vaudès, or Waldo, also took up apostolic poverty after having been impressed by the story of St. Alexis from the fourth century. After acquiring a sizable following due to the example of his life, he started to criticize the Roman Catholic clergy of his time. In opposition to the archbishop of Lyons, who forbade him and his followers to preach against the priesthood, he replied by declaring that they should follow God rather than men, echoing the words of the apostle Peter in Acts 5:29 some 1100 years earlier. By this determined declaration Valdes refused to bow to church authority.[16]

Even Thomas Aquinas (1225–74), the model theologian and doctor of the Roman Catholic Church during the scholastic era, held to a view very much compatible with *sola Scriptura*. As an answer to the first question in the *Summa Theologiae*, Aquinas writes:

> Nevertheless, sacred doctrine makes use of these authorities as extrinsic and probable arguments; but properly uses the authority of the canonical Scriptures as an incontrovertible proof, and the authority of the doctors of the Church as one that may properly be used, yet merely as probable. For our faith rests upon the revelation made to the apostles and prophets who wrote the

---

15. Frassetto, *Great Medieval Heretics*, 48–49.
16. Frassetto, *Great Medieval Heretics*, 68, 70.

## THE HISTORICAL DEVELOPMENT OF SOLA SCRIPTURA

canonical books, and not on the revelations (if any such there are) made to other doctors.[17]

Here Aquinas is admitting to the fact that the Scriptures have binding authority on the conscience of men. Even though the doctors of the church may have authority within the church, their authority is only probable, not certain. Aquinas says that the basis of our faith is the Scriptures, and no other.

Later, John Wycliffe (1324?–84), the learned Oxford theologian, stated in his work on the Scriptures:

> For since the whole of sacred scripture is the word of God, there could not be a superior, safer or more effective testimony than this: if God who cannot lie says this in his scripture, which is the mirror of his will, then it is true.[18]

This way, Wycliffe identifies the Scripture as the unsurpassable word of God. There is nothing on par with Scripture, neither tradition nor church authority. For Wycliffe, the Bible was the source of all true doctrines, and the law of the church. It was the final and absolute authority, and if the church did not adhere to its teachings, the church itself lost its authority. For example, Wycliffe rejected the teaching of transubstantiation based on his interpretation of the Scripture.

Wycliffe's teachings influenced Jan Hus (1369–1415) of Bohemia in the fifteenth century. Hus was an esteemed theologian and church leader in Prague, who led the drive in Bohemia to the return to the simple purity of the Bible as opposed to the secularism of the Roman Catholic Church in his day. Hus interpreted the words in Matt 16:18–19, "You are Peter, and on this rock I shall build my church,"[19] that the church was founded not on Peter himself but on his recognition of Jesus as the Son of God. Hus believed that Jesus Christ was the foundation of the church, and to claim otherwise was to turn biblical authority on its head. For Hus the Bible was the supreme authority, and not the opinions of fallen men.[20]

It was Martin Luther (1483–1546) who gave full and wide expression to the ultimate authority of the Scriptures. Luther rejected the teaching on

---

17. Aquinas, *Summa Theologiae*, 1a.1.8.

18. Frassetto, *Great Medieval Heretics*, 169.

19. The verse used by Rome as the foundation of the papacy, beginning with the apostle Peter.

20. Frassetto, *Great Medieval Heretics*, 193.

indulgences, saying it was contrary to the Scriptures during his hearing before Cardinal Cajetan and when he opposed Johann Eck's treatise on papal indulgences. As we can see with Luther and others before him, he chose to follow the Scriptures because they taught right living, in stark contradiction to the false teachings and immoral lives, avarice and simony that were prevalent during the Middle Ages.

In his treatise titled "Resolution Concerning the Authority of the Pope," Luther claimed that the papacy existed by the will of God but had no special sacred status. Furthermore, the pope was neither infallible nor had the final authority in the interpretation of the Scriptures.

For Luther, the Bible was the sole ultimate basis for his theology. This is because in it we can find the gospel of Jesus Christ, which teaches us how we can be saved and how we must live. For Luther, this was the central teaching of Christianity, and to go against the Scriptures would be most unwise. This is what was behind his purported words at the Diet of Worms in 1521:

> Since your most serene majesty and your lordships require of me a simple, clear and direct answer, I will give one, and it is this: Unless I am convinced by the testimony of the Scriptures and by clear reason (for I do not trust in the pope or councils alone, since it is well known that they have often erred and contradicted themselves), I am bound by the Scriptures I have quoted. My conscience is captive to the Word of God. I cannot and I will not retract anything, since it is neither safe nor right to go against conscience. Here I stand. I cannot do otherwise. God help me. Amen.[21]

John Calvin (1509–64) provides a detailed description of the authority of Scripture in the *Institutes*. Calvin makes a distinction between general revelation found in nature, which is capable of leading us only to the knowledge that God is, and the special revelation of God's character in the Bible. He compares it to giving a pair of glasses to a man who is shortsighted so he can see clearly. However, since man so easily forgets what he has learned about God the Creator from nature, that is why God chose to reveal himself via the written word. This way Calvin rejects any idea of nature being the sixty-seventh book of the Bible, as expounded by theistic evolutionists. God does not speak every day from the sky; that is why he left us a written record of his will.

---

21. Bainton, *Here I Stand*, 144.

Calvin repudiates the idea that the church has any authority to give us the Bible. He refers to Eph 2:20: "And are built upon the foundation of the apostles and prophets, Jesus Christ himself being the chief corner stone." Whereas the New Testament may indeed be founded by the apostles, however, the prophets of the Old Testament are also named, who represent the Old Testament, who preceded the Roman Catholic Church.

For Calvin, the Bible is a truly divinely inspired book without any equal. Though the books of the great writers of antiquity, Cicero, Plato, or Aristotle, are worth reading, yet they do not reach the grandeur and majesty of the word of God.

The Bible is full of thoughts that surely cannot have sprung from the mind of man.

Calvin writes that it is by the testimony of the Holy Spirit working in the believer that assures him of the truth and authority of the Scripture, above any kind of probabilistic considerations. Calvin uses the phrase αὐτόπιστον (*autopiston*) to denote the *self-authenticating* nature of the Scripture. As J. I. Packer notes, Scripture is self-authenticating, as an effective work of the Holy Spirit; therefore it is not right to subject the Bible to verification and arguments.[22]

This is a very important thing to note. The Bible does not need our support in interpreting it. The Bible isn't true just because we lend it our authority. The Bible doesn't derive its authority from human authority—much more the other way around. While the church is charged with handing down the (true) "tradition" of the gospel, problems arise when the church owns the gospel message for itself and makes changes to it on its own authority.

In 2 Sam 6:1–7 we read about how King David was transporting the ark of the covenant up from the house of Abinadab to his house. Uzzah and Ahio, the sons of Abinadab, were accompanying the ark when the oxen stumbled. Viscerally, Uzzah reached out to support the ark with his sinful hand but was struck dead by the Lord. This means that the Bible does not depend in any way on human intelligence in interpreting it. How could it if it is God's word?

Calvin also had to deal with people who could be compared to the modern charismatic movement, and who declared that they were taught directly by the Holy Spirit and had no need for the "dead letter" of the Bible, as Calvin described them. This shows that historically, there is

---

22. Packer, *Fundamentalism*, 121.

nothing new under the sun, and that the struggle to uphold *sola Scriptura* is the same as the struggles in the past.[23]

Both Luther and Calvin derived the authority of the Scriptures from its infallible nature. The Scriptures were infallible because they were God's word. Men such as popes and councils can err, but God never errs. In this way Luther tied *sola Scriptura* to *solus Christus*.[24]

Last, John Knox of England (1514–72) argued from the Bible, showing that the apostles Peter and Paul, besides Jesus Christ himself, referred their opponents to the Scriptures to test whether their doctrine was from God or not (John 5, 7; Acts 17; 2 Pet 1). He based his understanding of *sola Scriptura* on Deut 12:32: "Whatever I command you, be careful to observe it; you shall not add to it nor take away from it." Only that religion that can be verified by the Scriptures is acceptable. We are neither to add nor subtract anything to or from the Scriptures based on our own human wisdom.[25] Many consider Knox to be the guiding hand behind the Scottish *Book of Discipline* and the *Scots' Confession*, which upheld the doctrine of *sola Scriptura*. Whereas Knox did admit the authority of conscience, it was not enough if it lacked scriptural support. Furthermore, Knox also made room for the influence of denominational tradition, but he derived its authority from Scripture, and not vice versa as the church of Rome teaches. As to ecclesiastical authority, the church has authority only to oppose heresy, but it cannot formulate new articles of faith, nor give authority to Scripture.[26]

It is my hope that we can learn from what has transpired in the past so that we can more effectively address problems in the present.

---

23. Calvin, *Institutes*, 1.1.6–10.
24. Woodbridge, *Biblical Authority*, 52–57.
25. Knox, *Selected Writings*, 172, 453, 537.
26. Greaves, *Theology and Reformation*, 5–11.

# What Is *Sola Scriptura*?

Sanctify them by Your truth. Your word is truth.
JOHN 17:17

### Introduction, Epistemology, Definition

TO DELVE INTO THIS topic further, it would be most fitting to define the term *sola Scriptura* right at the beginning. First, I think that any serious student of the Bible should know what the term *sola Scriptura* means and be able to explain it. Second, one should be able to defend the teaching of *sola Scriptura* by citing at least five verses from the Bible that support it, even if woken up in the middle of the night. Third, one should also be able to apply the teaching of *sola Scriptura* to different doctrines and denominations to tell the difference between truth and falsehood. In deciding what is true or false, our epistemology defines for us what we are bound to do by our conscience.

*Sola Scriptura* is the epistemology of the Christian religion. Epistemology is a part of any discipline or knowledge system by which we can discern what is true and what is false, and why it is true or false. Without epistemology, a system is worth nothing, since any statement could be true and false at the same time, and no progress would be made whatsoever.[1]

We can define *sola Scriptura* in the following way: "The entire Bible alone, and not our own or anyone else's human interpretation of it, as illuminated by the Holy Spirit, is the sole highest divine authority in defining

---

1. This is a deep-seated problem characteristic of the charismatic movement, for example, which lacks a coherent, well-defined theology, due to the myriads of different and often contradicting charismatic churches.

truth for all people in New Testament times in all subject matter." This sentence is a bit lengthy but is descriptive enough to counteract many of the theological systems that oppose it. A shorthand way of defining *sola Scriptura* is that "the Bible is the sole highest authority."

The word *sola* in the Latin term *sola Scriptura* stands for "sole," or alone. This is a key concept here. This means that the Scripture is the sole form of untainted divine revelation given to us by God. The Bible stands alone as a form of divine revelation among other forms of supposed revelation or authorities, which may take many different forms. These other forms of revelation or authority include things such as tradition, church authority, which is characteristic of the Roman Catholic Church. Other forms of authority are characteristic of other religions, philosophies, sects, or cults: modern science for theistic evolution, philosophy, experientialism for the charismatic movement, or the writings of Ellen G. White, which Adventists suppose are a correct interpretation of the Bible.

In other words, *sola Scriptura* states that no other form of authority can compete with the Scriptures. The Scriptures are declared to have the final, highest authority, the last say in all matters. This means that all other forms of authority are under Scripture and are subservient to it. In fact, the presence of any other form of authority or revelation must necessarily be man made and is a telltale sign that it is being used as a vehicle by a cult or false religion to introduce their own extra-biblical teaching next to, or in place of, that of the Bible.

What differentiates the Scriptures from all other forms of authority is that only the Scriptures are purely divine. All other forms of authority are tainted with some marks of human opinion in them. This is very important because if one seeks the truth, one must make sure a perfect, infallible, inerrant tool is being used to determine the truth. If the source of authority someone is following has been shown to err in one place or another, then it becomes a legitimate question as to whether it has erred in another place. You cannot use a map with the wrong street names to get around in a city. Thus, since many people have been convinced by evolutionary theory into thinking that Genesis is false because it is unscientific, then they reject the rest of the Bible as well. The struggle of theological liberalism is thus a forlorn, ever-losing fight.

Along this note of divine authority, some churches or philosophies commit one of two classes of errors. First, some churches may elevate either their own authority or traditions to a divine level. This is making a man into God and is blasphemy. The Roman Catholic Church errs when she claims that her tradition and her church have binding authority. Others try to demote the word of God to the level of mere mortal humans. In this way, part of or even the entire Bible may err. This is characteristic of liberal theology.

Based on this we must heed the injunction of Scripture: "For I testify to everyone who hears the words of the prophecy of this book: If anyone adds to these things, God will add to him the plagues that are written in this book; and if anyone takes away from the words of the book of this prophecy, God shall take away his part from the Book of Life, from the holy city, and from the things which are written in this book" (Rev 22:18–19).

We may never add our own human wisdom to the Scriptures, purporting ourselves to be gods. Furthermore, we must also not detract from God's word, thereby making out God to be a liar or a dunce. This is another form of deifying man, by saying that a mere man can correct God.

## How Does *Sola Scriptura* Relate to the Other Four *Solas*?

*Sola Scriptura* is the epistemology of the Christian faith; thus it is the basis of the entire religion. Whatever man decides to be true must pass the filter of the Bible. If it doesn't, then it must be rejected, and it cannot stand. All the other four *solas*, *sola fide* (faith alone), *sola gratia* (grace alone), *solus Christus* (Christ alone), and *soli Deo gloria* (all glory to God) are Christian doctrines together with their practical meanings derived from Scripture. We infer from the Scriptures as the sole highest authority that salvation is by Christ alone and grace alone, received by faith alone. Therefore, the Christian will give all honor and glory to God alone. *Sola Scriptura* is basal in respect to these doctrines.

For a depiction of how the five Solas interrelate with one another, see fig. 1. This setup is important because theory determines practice, and not the other way around. Our truth does not define God's truth. Our truth is not even on the same level as God's truth. This is a key concept to remember.

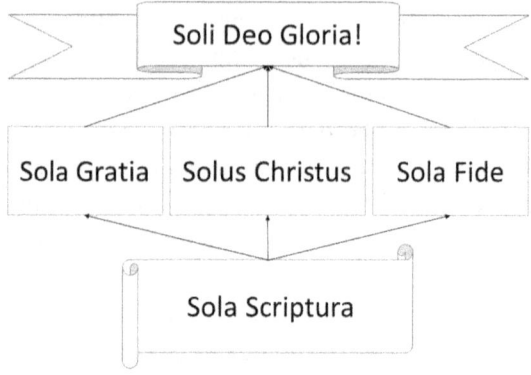

Figure 1. The relationship between the five Solas of the Reformation with *sola Scriptura* as the foundation of all Christian doctrine.

### Inerrancy and Infallibility

It is of vital importance today to discuss the inerrancy and the infallibility of the Bible in the light of modern scientific theories (such as evolution), which undermines the authority of Scripture. If the Bible errs even in one single part, then it lacks all authority in the whole. As such, if the Bible is errant, then the teaching of *sola Scriptura* is destroyed. This is even more important, since whole seminaries, even famous ones, such as Fuller Theological Seminary in California, have jettisoned the importance of the doctrines of biblical infallibility and inerrancy, to the detriment of the church. This is part and parcel of an insidious form of liberalism infecting the modern evangelical church. Even theologians within and without the church, such as Clark Pinnock, Peter Enns, Kenton Sparks, Kevin Vanhoozer, Andrew McGowan, Stanley Grenz, Brian McLaren, Darrell Bock, and Robert Webb, have all distorted or denied biblical inerrancy to various extents.[2]

Two important terms when dealing with the authority of the Bible are inerrancy and infallibility. Infallibility and inerrancy may be distinguished but not separated.[3] *Inerrancy* means that the Bible does not contain any mistakes or errors. This means that everything in the Bible is factually true. If the Bible makes an error in one place, how do we know

---

2. Geisler and Roach, *Defending Inerrancy*, 23.
3. International Council on Biblical Inerrancy, "Chicago Statement," art. 11.

that it has not made an error in another place?[4] "God is not a man that He should lie" (Num 23:19). The Spirit of God never makes false statements but guides us into all truth (John 16:13).

In contrast, the term "infallibility" is stronger than inerrancy. *Infallibility* means that *by its very nature* the Bible cannot err.[5] Even though the Bible is inerrant, the authors may have introduced errors into the Bible by nature. Therefore, when speaking about the inerrancy of the Bible, it is also important to add that the Bible is also infallible. This means that, by nature, the Bible cannot err in anything at any time whatsoever. The Bible is a perfect document.

But even with infallibility we must distinguish how far its scope extends. It is one thing to say that the Bible is infallible only in matters of faith and morals. It is another to say that the Bible is infallible in all things, even scientific statements. The first statement restricts biblical infallibility to only certain parts of the Bible. Some parts may be infallible, others may not. Liberal theologians are quick to say that the Bible is not trustworthy in scientific matters.

This, however, leads us back to inerrancy. If the Bible is infallible only in some parts, then in other parts it may make errors. This means that though the Bible may be infallible in faith and morals, it may still be errant in other parts. The whole Bible is the word of God; it doesn't only contain the word of God.[6] The Bible is true and trustworthy in all matters that it speaks of; there is no bound or limit.[7]

Even the field of mathematics is not neutral. You may think that as a subject, math describes nature in only a neutral fashion. Mathematics described in this matter suggests that human logic and reasoning can determine anything, which is the falsehood our first parents believed in the garden.[8] However, when the Reformers spoke about mathematics, they approached it with the understanding that it recorded the truth God had created and sustains in the natural world. Math and logic were created by God and given to us to help understand nature in order to subdue and rule over it (Gen 1:28).[9]

---

4. Geisler, *Inerrancy*, 81.
5. Crampton, *By Scripture Alone*, 77.
6. Kistler, *Sola Scriptura*, 88–89.
7. International Council on Biblical Inerrancy, "Chicago Statement," art. 9, 11.
8. Loop, *Beyond Numbers*, 46.
9. Loop, *Beyond Numbers*, 37, 47.

Were Jesus and the apostles accurate when Jesus spoke of scientific matters? Jesus mentions the Genesis flood in Matt 24:37–39. Certain modern theories of geology deny that the flood ever happened. Who is right? Jesus or the men whom he created (since He is God)? One could reason that since Jesus created these men, he should know more than what they do. As such, we should trust Jesus' divine knowledge rather than the fallible theories of men.

Some may point out that Jesus as a man did not know all things, since in v. 36, only the Father knows the hour of Jesus' coming. This may be so, but it is also true that Jesus did know about the Genesis flood, since he spoke about it. Jesus was infallible in whatever matter he spoke about. "Heaven and earth will pass away, but My words will by no means pass away" (Matt 24:35).

**The Word of God Is Sufficient**

In this dark world the word of God is "a lamp unto my feet and a light unto my path" (Ps 119:105). It is also like a great big house, within which the man of God hears God's voice and understands his will. "All Scripture is given by inspiration of God, and is profitable for doctrine, for reproof, for correction, for instruction in righteousness: that the man of God may be perfect, thoroughly furnished unto all good works" (2 Tim 3:26–27).

In this sense the Bible is enough for the man of God to live a full, godly, spiritual, and effective life in the service of the Lord. This is a very important issue. If a man for some reason thinks that there must be more to life than the word of God, then this leads to a denial of the sufficiency of Scripture, and with it a denial of the principle of *sola Scriptura*. If we look to anything other than the word of God, then in reality we are turning to the authority of men, and this is a sign of lack of trust in God's word.

Does this sound like what is called a fortress mentality? Some define fortress mentality as a sort of blind unwillingness to go outside of the house of God, and to consider the things of the world. According to this, a fortress mentality means that to gain a convert we briefly break out of our fortress into the world, take our hostage, and bring him back to safety behind the walls of the fortress.

But how can a "fortress mentality" be wrong if what God provides for us in his word is more than sufficient? This is a false mentality and is a sign of a lack of faith. Psalm 18:2 says: "The Lord is my rock, and my fortress, and my deliverer; my God, my strength, in whom I will trust; my buckler, and the horn of my salvation, and my high tower." Psalm 71:3 says: "Be my strong refuge, To which I may resort continually; You have given the commandment to save me, For You are my rock and my fortress." Other verses that describe God as a fortress include 2 Sam 22:2; Ps 31:3; 91:2; 144:2; Jer 6:27; 16:19. The Bible thus clearly advocates for a fortress mentality!

Matthew 7:24–27 describes the parable of building upon rock and upon stone. According to vv. 24–25:

> Therefore whosoever heareth these sayings of mine, and doeth them, I will liken him unto a wise man, which built his house upon a rock: And the rain descended, and the floods came, and the winds blew, and beat upon that house; and it fell not: for it was founded upon a rock.

Such a rock is the word of God. It does not need to be augmented, propped up, or verified. It is self-authenticating. If we follow the word of God, we surely cannot go wrong. But Jesus describes the man who builds upon the sand, the shifting sands of man's opinion: "And the rain descended, and the floods came, and the winds blew, and beat upon that house; and it fell: and great was the fall of it."

In other words, to go past the Bible in search of other sources of revelation is futile. By disregarding the Bible, we are going outside of the fortress, and *away from the Bible*. Such a thought should strike peril into our hearts. Yet so many denominations that call themselves Christian do it all the time, and even entice other Christians inadvertently to leave the solid foundation that is the word of God.

Those philosophies and movements that hold a low view of the Bible also tend to have a false hermeneutic, and thus a false view of the authority of Scripture as well. In other words, if someone does not believe the Bible to be sufficient, they will turn to other sources to supplement God's word.[10] These include certain origin theories, church authority, mystical experience, or others. In the next chapters many false views of scriptural authority will be examined and refuted. This also means that if these philosophies have the need to supplement God's word, they also have at least a partially false view of God himself.

---

10. Geisler and Roach, *Defending Inerrancy*, 282–83.

### What Does *Sola Scriptura* Not Mean?

Just as so many people in the church do not understand what *sola Scriptura* is, it is also very common for people to attach incorrect meanings to this concept. In this way, I listened to how a radio talk show host declared on the air that he thought that *sola Scriptura* was wrong, besides giving an incorrect definition of it. This particular radio host thought that *sola Scriptura* means that the Bible is the only authority in the world. We shall see why this is not the case, and that this definition does not match the definition of *sola Scriptura*.

We defined *sola Scriptura* as the Bible being the sole highest authority over all other sources of authority subordinate to it. However, we must not necessarily conclude that all other forms of authority are useless. For example, the Bible says, "Obey those who rule over you, and be submissive, for they watch out for your souls, as those who must give account. Let them do so with joy and not with grief, for that would be unprofitable for you" (Heb 13:17).

If you ever get sick, you would certainly listen to your doctor's medical authority and take whatever medication he prescribes to you to get better. As another example, the bacterium *Bacillus subtilis* is not mentioned in the Bible; we just accept that it exists due to the authority of taxonomy.

The error that *only the Bible contains all knowledge* is called *solo Scriptura*. This is false, because we know that the Bible doesn't speak about many things.

All other authorities are *relative* to the Bible. This means that they can be accepted *only if they do not contradict the Bible*, which has the final say in all questions for all people throughout all time. If something contradicts the Bible, then we know that it must be wrong. This is the practical application of *sola Scriptura*. For example, since evolutionary theories say that men evolved from apes, and that the earth is 4.5 billion years old, we must reject them, since the Bible says that God created everything in the space of six, regular, twenty-four-hour days and that he created man in his image, separately from all other kinds of animals (Gen 1:5, 26–28).

In other words, these relative authorities form a hierarchy, with the Scriptures being the sole highest authority above all other sources. This is depicted in fig. 2.

## WHAT IS SOLA SCRIPTURA?

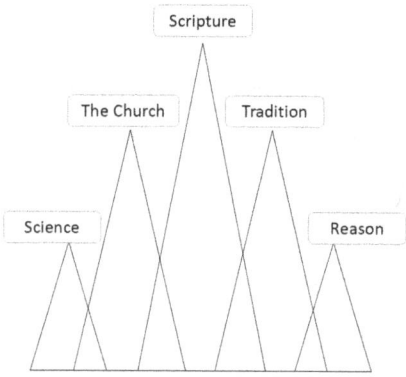

Figure 2. The Scriptures are the sole highest authority above all other relative authorities. Only the words of Scripture are absolute and unchanging, subject to no kind of criticism.

From a Roman Catholic viewpoint, it is important to note here that the content of the Bible is determined by the process of *canonization*. Imagine a hypothetical computer program, which takes as input all the writings of the Jews and the early church and applies an algorithm to determine which books or writings belong to the canon, and which do not. The algorithm can be anything we want, since the selection of the canon of the Bible itself is not infallible.[11] Next, doctrines are extracted from the Bible by the process of hermeneutics, which may also have a variety of different rules. *Sola Scriptura* is a *principle* that determines that the source with the single highest authority for hermeneutics is the Bible. But it doesn't touch upon what the proper content of the Bible itself is.

This process just described is somewhat akin to sculpting a statue. Whereas the sculptor may use chisels, picks, hammers, drills, or whatnot as tools to start sculpting the statue from its raw material (hermeneutics), choosing the material for the statue (clay, cement, metal, etc.) is akin to selecting what sources we use to make the statue out of. *Sola Scriptura* would be something like saying that we are sculpting a statue out of cement only, but with the possibility of using several tools to make the statue. The fact that we use cement only means that we use the Scripture alone as our basis for doctrine.

---

11. Kistler, *Sola Scriptura*, 66–67.

Here I must issue a warning to those who might seek to justify their own actions or views by stating that since it is not explicitly mentioned in the Bible, they are free to hold to that particular view. The Bible does say many things on many subjects, and presents to the reader a complete worldview dealing with a wide variety of issues, including politics, economics, law, and even science. The Christian believer must take care to have a thorough knowledge of the Bible, and study it regularly and in depth. The proper attitude is that our thinking must be rooted in and start out from the Bible. In this way, we will always know what is pleasing to God, and what is in accordance with his will (Rom 12:1–2).

### What about Statements of Faith and Catechisms?

For some it might seem surprising to say (regarding the topic and the main thrust of this book) that having statements of faith and teaching catechisms is perfectly acceptable, albeit subordinate to the Scriptures. Paul writes in 2 Thess 2:15: "Therefore, brethren, stand fast, and *hold the traditions* which ye have been taught, whether by word, or our epistle." Naturally, these traditions must rest on Scripture. Man-made traditions made up in a vacuum are unacceptable.

Many Christians today are focused on the idea that they must live out a "God and me" mentality. They fail to recognize that the church is made up of more than one single individual, and that worship happens in a corporate setting. In other words, while it is true that Christians must practice a deep, personal relationship with God, they must also practice worshiping God in a corporate manner. In other words, it is "God and *us*." The Holy Spirit works among believers as a community. Individual believers cannot live isolated from one another.

Many Christians approach the Bible with the mentality that you should read it as if nobody tells you anything about it, meaning that you shouldn't let anyone influence your thoughts when you read the Bible. This train of thought is based on Western anti-authoritarianism. This is wrong, because it then rejects the fact that the Holy Spirit has guided millions of godly men and women to the truth all throughout the six millennia of church history. In fact, one can be pretty sure that if someone comes up with a radically new idea, a new doctrine, a new fad, or a new method of worship or evangelization that the church never taught, then they are in error. According to the saying, "If it's new, it's not true; and if it's true, it's not new."

The church has existed all throughout time. Its teaching is (or ideally should be) constant and unwavering. As such, this church that has always existed ever since the garden of Eden when the first gospel (the protevangelion [Gen 3:15]) was preached to Adam and Eve. This church is called rightly the catholic church, because it encompasses believers of all nations, tribes, people groups, in all times.[12] The term "catholic" comes from the Greek word καθόλου (*katholou*), which means wholeness, entirety, or according to the whole, that is, the whole church.[13] By the work of the Holy Spirit who leads believers into all truth (John 16:13), the truth has been preserved in the catholic church.

The fact that there are so many denominations is because of sin. If we could eradicate sin here on this earth, then there would be only one denomination. But since nobody will ever be perfect here on earth, our minds will always be clouded by sin, and we will always misinterpret Scripture. If there was anyone whose mind was unclouded by sin, we wouldn't need the Bible!

According to *sola Scriptura*, you cannot put any kind of man-made tradition on par with Scripture. In this way, the more denominational churches, which have been around for centuries, are doing nothing wrong in writing down what they believe and asking their membership to adhere to it. After all, according to the fallacy of *solo Scriptura*, the Bible doesn't talk about everything. We could even venture so far as to say that a longer catechism is a sign that the given church body has a lot to say about God, even to say that those churches have a deeper knowledge of God. We shouldn't shy away from writing down what we believe. The Apostle's Creed is a statement of faith unabashedly held by all Christian denominations. According to the ideas of Cornelius van Til, we are thinking God's thoughts after him.[14]

This, of course, is only permissible inasmuch as these catechisms are treated with their proper respect, keeping in mind that catechisms and statements of faith are relative authorities in respect to the Scriptures.[15] The Westminster Confession of Faith, a Presbyterian source, states the following:

---

12. The catholic church is totally unrelated to the Roman Catholic Church. Rome misappropriates the title catholic to herself.
13. Williams, *Evangelicals and Tradition*, 16.
14. Van Til, *Christian Apologetics*, 140.
15. Allen, *Sola*, 20.

> The supreme judge by which all controversies of religion are to be determined, and all decrees of councils, opinions of ancient writers, doctrines of men, and private spirits, are to be examined, and in whose sentence we are to rest, can be no other but the Holy Spirit speaking in the Scripture.[16]

Regarding the role of the Holy Spirit in speaking to us through the Scriptures, several points must be made. The Holy Spirit is the Spirit of truth (John 16:13) and will provide a good hermeneutic for us. We have to do the hard work of thinking and understanding. The Holy Spirit will also never lead us to an understanding that is contrary to the word of God. Neither will the Holy Spirit reveal to us anything new that is not found in the pages of Scripture. Last, the Holy Spirit will also never bypass the text of Scripture. These things are all particularly relevant when we discuss the charismatic movement.[17]

Applying *sola Scriptura* to a catechism or a statement of faith itself means that if the catechism in any point contradicts the Bible, then the catechism must be amended. A church that has a healthy relationship with the Scriptures should be able to change any part of its statement of faith at any time if it is found to contradict the Scriptures. The sign of a good confession is if it comports with Scripture, and a bad confession is one that does not. We should also note here that we do not require men to hold to confessions, because only the Scriptures can bind the conscience, not confessions. However, at the same time, since we humans do not know the Bible inside and out, we adhere to confessions, simply as part of being human.

Some claim that they have "no creed but Christ," and no confession but the Bible. Their attitude is commendable, but in reality, it is something that cannot be attained in this life. If we did, and if our confession truly is the Bible only, then this means that our opinions on matters line up perfectly with the Bible. In line with the principle of *sola Scriptura*, it is something that we should attain, knowing at the same time that, due to our finiteness, we will attain full knowledge only in eternity.

## Christian Freedom

Since the Bible doesn't talk about everything, this leaves a lot of freedom for the Christian. At their meetings Quakers would speak only if they felt that

---

16. Westminster Confession of Faith 1.10, M. Smith, *Harmony*, 15.
17. Geisler and Roach, *Defending Inerrancy*, 294.

the Spirit of God was moving upon them. Others would get out of bed in the morning only if they could discern that God was telling them to do so. Christians need not go to such extremes. We have freedom! God may not tell us exactly what brand of shoes to buy at the store. He may not tell us which Christian movie to watch. He leaves it to his children as a gift!

God gave us his word. If we understand his word, we will understand the way God thinks. If we put his word into practice, we will be more like Christ. As Christians, we need to know discerningly how to use God's word in whatever life situation comes up.

## Pragmatism

Another important issue to cover when dealing with the topic of *sola Scriptura* is that of pragmatism. Pragmatism means that we do what we think works for us in a given situation. As such, it is man centered, and not focused on God. It belies a lack of trust in God's providence and God's word. Its starting point is man's experience, and what man thinks is good. It is easy for many people to think in a pragmatic way.

In Roman Catholicism, pragmatism leads to false worship. In the charismatic movement, it leads to false ways of evangelization. In liberalism, it leads to the acceptance of false ideologies, such as theistic evolution.

## *Sola Scriptura* and Worship

The denial of *sola Scriptura* can also be seen in a practical manner, namely in how we worship God. This has serious practical consequences. The way we approach God for salvation and how we worship him are bound up with one another. Just how we cannot simply invent our own rules as to how we can be saved, so also, we cannot make up our own way of how we worship him.

Jesus says in Matt 7:21–23: "Not everyone who says to Me, 'Lord, Lord,' shall enter the kingdom of heaven, but he who does the will of My Father in heaven. Many will say to Me in that day, 'Lord, Lord, have we not prophesied in Your name, cast out demons in Your name, and done many wonders in Your name?' And then I will declare to them, 'I never knew you; depart from Me, you who practice lawlessness!'"

Many people think that they do well when in reality they are seeking only themselves and not God's glory. They think they can buy God off with their own good deeds in exchange for salvation. They are not considering what God has set down in his word as to how we must truly worship him. Since the Scriptures are God's self-revelation, the Scriptures must inform us about a right conception of God, which is essential in how we must worship him.

The story of the golden calf (Exod 32) accurately describes worshipping God in a false manner outside of the Scriptures. While Moses is busy on Mount Sinai receiving the Ten Commandments from the Lord, the people in the camp below are getting impatient with him. They ask Aaron to make a god for them to go before them. Aaron then takes their gold and forms a molten calf, claiming that this is the god who brought them from Egypt. The idolatry of the Israelites consisted not in their worshipping an entirely false god, but rather in portraying God in a degrading manner.[18] Worse, they broke the Second Commandment, which prohibits depicting God in any form. The golden calf incident was an example of breaking the principle of *sola Scriptura* with regards to worship.

Leviticus is a book in the Old Testament that focuses on how the Jews were to worship God. In Lev 10:1–2 we read, "Then Nadab and Abihu, the sons of Aaron, each took his censer and put fire in it, put incense on it, and offered profane fire before the Lord, which He had not commanded them. So fire went out from the Lord and devoured them, and they died before the Lord." This passage of Scripture illustrates that Aaron's two sons, Nadab and Abihu, thought that they were worthy to bring their own fire for offering in the tabernacle in the Israelite camp. They were consumed by fire. What God does not command in worship, that he also does not accept.

This principle is illustrated in the way that Luther and Calvin tried to reform Roman Catholic worship. Luther's principle was to dispatch with each such element of worship that was not found in Scripture. In comparison, Calvin went even further in that he first emptied the church and brought in only those elements that were expressly commanded in Scripture. For Calvin, no element of worship is neutral. In other words, there are no adiaphora.[19]

In this way, the broader evangelical church has gone astray. It has introduced false worship due to the practical denial of *sola Scriptura*. Rock music is also a common element in evangelical churches. This is a problem, since rock music was invented by secular musicians; according to

18. Alexander, *From Paradise*.
19. A Greek term for "indifferent things."

one secular rock musician, rock music is "99% sex."[20] Furthermore, some churches have introduced different forms of entertainment to attract and keep people in their church. Some churches have gone so far that pastors even hold wrestling matches during the service for entertainment.

There is a lot of work to do in reforming the church today.

## Tota Scriptura

Another term that is closely related to *sola Scriptura* is called *tota Scriptura*, otherwise known as *plenary inspiration* or *verbal inspiration*. Plenary inspiration means that every single verse in the Bible is inspired by God.[21] Each verse has exactly the same weight as any other verse.[22] Verses cannot be pitted against one another, as though one verse takes precedence or negates another verse. This also means that there are no contradictions in the Bible. Every single verse must be taken into account when interpreting Scripture so that they harmonize with one another. You will understand a given doctrine in the Bible only if you see it in its entirety, in full detail.

This concept serves as a safeguard against isolating a single Bible verse, taking it out of its context, and using it in precedence against the rest of the Bible. If one single verse from the Bible is backed by divine authority, then all other verses in the Bible have the same kind of divine backing. This is why the famous verse from 2 Tim 3:16 begins in this way: "*All scripture* is given by inspiration of God." The principle of *tota Scriptura* means that the entire Bible is God's word, not just bits and pieces of it. *Tota Scriptura* says that the whole Scripture, and all its parts, down to the very words of the original, were given by divine inspiration.

Furthermore, we cannot say that though the whole Bible is divinely inspired, without the parts; or that parts of Scripture are inspired, but not the whole.[23] Therefore, different parts of Scripture cannot be just simply jettisoned, or divided between different people groups during different time periods. This will be examined in the chapters dealing with dispensationalism and liberalism.

*Tota Scriptura* is an important principle in biblical exegesis, since we must look at what the *whole* Bible says about a given topic to determine

---

20. Cloud, *Rock Music*, 13.
21. Mueller, *Called to Believe*, 39.
22. In other words, every verse in the Bible has the same authority.
23. International Council on Biblical Inerrancy, "Chicago Statement," art. 6.

proper biblical teaching it. This is an important principle to remember because it deals with how the Bible relates to itself. When examining a specific theological issue, one cannot pit separate verses against each other or omit them. This is an unwholesome tendency of liberalism to criticize some parts of the Bible with others, tacitly denying the authority of the criticized portion of the Bible.[24] We need to take the whole Bible into account when exegeting a specific question.

**The Exclusivity of *Sola Scriptura***

It would be worth comparing the different sacred writings of different world religions in our assessment of the principle of *sola Scriptura*. As we shall see, *sola Scriptura* is exclusive to the Judeo-Christian religion. This illustrates that the principle of *sola Scriptura* is unique to Christianity among all religions since Christianity is itself a unique religion. This is because only the religion of Christianity comes from God, because the Holy Scriptures themselves also come purely and entirely from God.

In contrast, let us first examine the religion of Judaism. Orthodox Judaism today is not the same as the Jewish religion of the Old Testament. This is because by and large modern Orthodox Judaism has added its own traditions to the Scripture, ever since the time of Christ. This is why Jesus upbraids the Pharisees in Mark 7:8 for laying aside the commandments of God in favor of their own traditions.

But in the beginning of Judaism this was not so. By the middle of the eighth century AD a group of Jewish believers called the Karaites (*Kara'im*) had broken away from the rest of Judaism. The Karaites held to the principle of *sola Scriptura* in that they held the Old Testament only as ultimately binding. The Karaites had two sayings that comport with the principle of *sola Scriptura*: "Search thoroughly in the Tanakh [the Old Testament] and do not rely on my opinion." Furthermore, "A rule in our tradition is that (which) is shown to be wrong on the basis of the written text, will not be accepted any more, for it is not considered as possessing divine sanctity."[25]

Table 1 below depicts the four different interpretations Orthodox Judaism attaches to individual Old Testament verses. They very much

---

24. Packer, *Fundamentalism*, 110.
25. Cserhati, *Refuting Rome*, 25–26.

resemble the fourfold interpretational system used by the Roman Catholic Church, following Origen and the medieval exegetes.[26]

Table 1. The fourfold interpretation of the Scripture in Orthodox Judaism and Roman Catholicism compared

|  | Orthodox Judaism | Roman Catholicism |
|---|---|---|
| Pe'shat (פְּשָׁט) | Literal sense | Literal sense |
| Remez (רֶמֶז) | Aggadic or allegorical sense | Allegorical sense |
| De'rash (דְּרָשׁ) | Admonitory, legal sense | Moral sense |
| Sod (סוֹד) | Kabbalistic mystical gnosis | Anagogic sense |

Besides this, Orthodox Judaism had developed a whole system of traditions by the time of Jesus as a supplement to the Old Testament:

- The Talmud: A commentary on the Old Testament
- The Mishnah: Judaic writings formed on oral tradition
- The Tosefta: Supplement to the Mishnah, along with additional traditions
- The Gemara: Exegetical writings about the Mishnah
- The kabbalistic *Zohar*: An occult gnostic synthesis of Pharaonic Egypt and ancient Babylon, considered to be the key to understanding the Pentateuch

These extra-biblical authorities as well as the fourfold way of interpreting Scripture illustrate the fact that the denial of *sola Scriptura* leads to humanism and the exaltation of tradition over God's word.

In comparison, in Islam, besides the Qur'an we have the Hadith, which are stories or oral traditions, which were later written down, of what Mohammed either said, did, or approved, which were either said or done when he was present. According to Kateregga and Schenk, as quoted by Geisler and Saleeb,

---

26. Packer, *Fundamentalism*, 103–4.

> The Hadith is not a Holy Book (revelation) as the Qur'an and the previous Scriptures. However, to the Muslims the importance of Hadith ranks only second to the Holy Qur'an. The Hadith is complementary to the Qur'an. It helps to explain and clarify the Holy Qur'an and to present the Qur'an in a more practical form. . . . As Muslims, our knowledge of Islam would be incomplete and shaky if we did not study and follow the Hadith. Similarly an outsider cannot understand Islam if he ignores the Hadith.[27]

Here we see that in Islam, a form of oral tradition, the Hadith, complements the holy book of Islam. Just as in Roman Catholicism, it seeks to clarify the written word. According to the author, Islam would not be complete without the Hadith of Mohammed. For example, the exact words of the Muslims' daily prayer, the *shahadah*, are not found in the Qur'an.[28] The Hadith has an impact on the way Muslims live in that they try to follow Mohammed's example as portrayed in the Hadith. Islamic law is based on the Qur'an, the Hadith, and *ijma* (the consensus of the community), as well as *qiyas*, which is the application of analogical reasoning to the previous three sources.[29]

Just as we have seen previously in Orthodox Judaism, in Islam we have secondary and postsecondary sources that are relied upon to interpret the previous, major sources, and which are relied upon to make important life decisions, such as laws. Interestingly, the Roman Catholic Church also has something that is similar to the *ijma* of Islam. It is called the *sensus fidei*, or the "sense of faith," which is defined as follows:

> The whole body of the faithful . . . cannot err in matters of belief. This characteristic is shown in the supernatural appreciation of faith (*sensus fidei*) on the part of the whole people, when, from the bishops to the last of the faithful, they manifest a universal consent in matters of faith and morals.[30]

In both cases we have man augmenting divine revelation with his own words, whether it complements the divine word or whether it makes man a reference of truth.

---

27. Geisler and Saleeb, *Answering Islam*, 83.
28. Qureshi, *No God but One*.
29. Geisler and Saleeb, *Answering Islam*, 84.
30. Interdicasterial Commission, *Catechism of Catholic Church*, para. 92.

## Why Do People Deviate from *Sola Scriptura*?

Last, it is important to discuss what reasons there are behind people deviating from *sola Scriptura*. In the following chapters we will look at several religions and movements in details to why they do so. But prior to that this issue may be discussed in general here.

One of the main reasons people deviate from *sola Scriptura* is a mistrust of God. Not understanding God, they wish to control him. The unknown strikes fear into people.[31] As such, people define the truth for themselves in their own way, in order to grasp at a seemingly firm foundation, irrespective of whether it overlaps with the Bible.

These are the reasons why people look to other forms of extra-biblical revelation, be it tradition, visions, scientific theories, experience, etc. This way people wish to feel secure in knowing the unknown. But this is only a false security because all other sources outside Scripture are fallible. Therefore, people make their own human understanding or experience the ultimate standard for all truth. This leads to humanism but also mysticism.

In this book, several false religions or false tendencies within the church will be examined. In doing this, the goal is not to attack adherents of these other viewpoints. Rather, we must lovingly identify the source of the problem that is inherent in these religions or denominations with the hope of reforming them after repentance.

---

31. Marston, *Voice of Authority*, 13.

# Extra-Biblical Revelation: The Charismatic Movement

> And he said unto him, If they do not hear Moses and the prophets, neither will they be persuaded though one rise from the dead.
> LUKE 16:31

### Introduction

BESIDES THE ROMAN CATHOLIC Church with its approximately one billion adherents worldwide, another major religious movement also adds a wide variety of extra-biblical sources of revelation to its repertoire. This is the charismatic movement, which claims around roughly five hundred million members worldwide, although it is very diverse and amorphous.

Characteristic of this historically recent movement (the beginning of the twentieth century) is that it was formed as a reaction against the decay of theological liberalism as well as atheism and materialism, which gained wide acceptance after the advent of evolutionary theory.[1] The charismatic movement could not endure what it felt was the spiritual dryness of some church environments. These people sought after, coveted church renewal, a revival stemming from fresh spiritual experiences. Thus, the charismatic movement made the human experience the measure of religious validity. This is humanism in just another guise.

Though charismatics falsely accuse evangelical Christians of rationalism, they themselves go back to a certain brand of humanism called empiricism, characterized by the philosophies of the British empiricists,

---

1. Masters and Whitcomb, *Charismatic Phenomenon*, 11.

such as John Locke, George Berkeley, or the atheist David Hume. These philosophers reacted to the continental rationalists of the seventeenth and eighteenth century who claimed that everything can be explained by logic and reason.[2] For them, something is really only meaningful and true if it can be perceived and experienced.[3] As one charismatic pastor put it, his opponent may have an argument, but he has an experience. In such a way, the charismatic movement divorced rationality and logic from an enthusiastic experience of God's love.

Parallel with this, in keeping with their new experientialism, they combat atheism by seeking to prove the existence of God by signs, wonders, miracles, and supernatural healings. "You want proof of God's existence?" they ask atheists—"We'll deliver you the evidence!"

In line with this is another elemental characteristic of the origin of the charismatic movement. This characteristic can be traced back to the times of Charles Finney, the famous preacher from the nineteenth century. Finney was completely sold on free-will Arminian theology—so much so that some classify him as full-blown Pelagian. Finney believed in something called "activating grace," which was a type of grace that came from God and which the preachers of the gospel could harness to "activate" faith latent in his unregenerate listeners.

According to Finney's beliefs, the preacher needed to pique peoples' interest in the gospel with intense, dramatic, gripping stories, such as how some people came to faith from their former lives steeped in sin, to make it easy for others to become Christian.[4] This is why when many charismatics tell you about their conversion story, there is a great deal of drama involved. This kind of thing is also widespread in noncharismatic churches as well.

This is also why the charismatic movement is so preoccupied with fighting against demons, because it is so dramatic and vivid. This is also why the charismatic movement, among other churches, is engrossed in end-time prophecies and charting out where we are exactly according to the timeline of the book of Revelation. This is because the future, the unknown, is so interesting, mesmerizing, and it captures many peoples' imagination if somehow we could know what will happen next before it actually comes to

---

2. Sahakian, *History of Philosophy*, 153–68.

3. Therefore, these philosophers would claim that if a tree fell down in a forest with nobody there, it would not make any sound at all, since nobody was there to hear the sound.

4. Reed, *Making Shipwreck of Faith*, 22–23.

pass. This is why a sort of carnival-like atmosphere is characteristic of some charismatic churches.[5]

One time my charismatic colleague told me that the period called the Great Tribulation was right around the corner (literally only two or three weeks), and that we needed to start preparing for this terrible time. Several months later, when nothing happened, I asked my colleague about it. He flat out denied that he had ever said it.

Things do happen in charismatic churches, but because they go beyond the Scriptures, the big question is, where do these things all come from?

The charismatic movement was more than ready, and indeed very willing, to move past the Scriptures and indulge in all sorts of spiritual experiences and manifestations, to the point of excess. In this way charismatics, just like liberals, outcompete each other in attempting the newest, the latest and greatest spiritual experiences. Hence the name enthusiasts, a synonym for charismatic.

Attending a charismatic church service, one gets the feeling that one is witnessing a spiritual carnival or circus. Many people come forth with spiritual testimonies, describing what God has done in their lives, or that they have received a "word from God." All of this goes back to the tradition of Charles Finney, the itinerant preacher who spoke of exciting the religious feelings of people so that God would be able to move about on them.

Some charismatics will then argue that the word that they think they received from God was meant only for them personally, and not for anyone else. But how can a word from God not edify others besides yourselves? Charismatics encourage each other to bear testimony about what God has said to them or what God has done in their lives. For example, the angel told Mary not to be afraid, since she had found favor with God (Luke 1:30). This was told to her alone explicitly, yet it became part of Luke's Gospel so that all could learn and be edified from it.

Just think about it. Who can possibly monitor what God supposedly tells five hundred million charismatics in private? If charismatic theology really is true, then what if God tells one man something that is absolutely necessary for salvation, but not known to the world? Isn't it good that everything you need for salvation is already in the Bible? No extra-biblical revelation needed.

---

5. The name of the Sunday service of a very prominent charismatic church, Hit Gyülekezete (The Faith Church), in Hungary is Vidámvasárnap (Happy Sunday).

# EXTRA-BIBLICAL REVELATION: THE CHARISMATIC MOVEMENT

Charismatics may claim that the "word" that they receive from God is not new revelation. However, it is important enough for them to base life decisions on these extra-biblical words, such as buying a house.[6] Since these "words" function as revelation in practice, this is merely a distinction without a difference.[7]

The charismatic movement cannot exist if *sola Scriptura* is valid, since as we have seen, the only valid source of divine revelation is the Scriptures. If *sola Scriptura* is true, then there is no charismatic movement. And, conversely, if the charismatic movement is right, then that means that the Scripture has no exclusive authority and can be disregarded—if God indeed does directly speak personally to all men, giving them extra-biblical revelation, then what need do we have of the Scripture as the primary authority?

Sadly, since the Bible is so consistently de-emphasized in the charismatic movement, this leads them into formulating doctrine that is opposed to the Scripture. For example, since charismatics believe that since the Holy Spirit can indwell and lead women, then women can become teachers and leaders in their churches, despite the clear biblical injunction: "But I suffer not a woman to teach, nor to usurp authority over the man, but to be in silence" (1 Tim 2:12), or that "*A bishop* then must be blameless, *the husband of one wife*, vigilant, sober, of good behaviour, given to hospitality, apt to teach" (1 Tim 3:2). Here bishop means the same thing as elder or presbyter (see Acts 20:17–28).

In the following we shall examine the extra-biblical sources of revelation that the charismatic movement claims as valid, and then we will examine them in the light of *sola Scriptura*.

## The Central Problem of the Charismatic Movement

As opposed to Roman Catholicism, which seeks to officially doctrinize its tradition and church authority, the charismatic movement plants its source of revelation squarely outside of the Bible and in the sensory mechanisms of the human being. The charismatics are trichotomists in that they believe that man is made up of body, soul, and spirit, the latter being a sort of organ connected to the Holy Spirit by which the charismatic individual communicates with him. Even though charismatics may seem unshakable in the kind of

---

6. A charismatic acquaintance of mine told me the reason he had bought his house for $247,000 was because he thought that the Holy Spirit wanted him to use that house 24/7.

7. Kistler, *Sola Scriptura*, 92.

experiences they have gained throughout their spiritual journeys, this kind of subjective experientialism undoes their whole worldview.

If human experience is the measuring rod of all truth, then what would ever happen if two charismatic individuals ever met up with each other, both of whom claimed that they had received a word from God, but which two separate messages were completely and mutually exclusive of one another? The problem we have here is that even though a charismatic person may think that he has an experience with which to go by, his experience is only subjective, that is, it is known only to himself. Another person can accept the truth of his experience based only on *the first person's authority* that he had that experience. In such a way, charismatic experientialism ends up generating thousands upon thousands of extrabiblical traditions as it goes along.

Even worse, since the only way we know what a self-proclaimed prophet is saying is true is purely by the "prophet's" authority, the person could well be lying. Anyone can make up anything. The Bible records such a case in 1 Kgs 13:9–24. A man of God has healed the hand of King Jeroboam and is on his way home. The Lord revealed to him that he must not stay to eat bread or drink water in that place (v. 9). He must go home immediately, without delay. However, an old man, a "prophet," finds out about the man of God's visit to the king and goes after him. He entices the man of God to come back and eat with him, claiming that the Lord revealed to him that he must do so. The Bible tells us that this false prophet was lying (v. 18). The man of God gives in and eats with the false prophet. Verse 24 describes how a lion comes and kills the man of God.

A solid Christian faith has the Scriptures to go by, since the Scriptures are available to all, whereby we can measure anything that another person says. In this way, the Scriptures are the sole source of objective truth. Accordingly, Scripture says, "The secret things belong to the Lord our God, but those things which are revealed belong to us and to our children forever, that we may do all the words of this law" (Deut 29:29).

In practice, charismatic churches go so far that individual charismatic churches reject one another's teachings based on their mutually contradictory experiences. Based on individual experiences and teachings the charismatic movement falls apart into individual atomistic church bodies, or "ecclesioles." Rome may point to the multitude of these "neo-Protestant" churches as evidence of the error of *sola Scriptura*,[8] but it is

---

8. It is only fair to compare Roman Catholic theory with Protestant theory, or Roman

## EXTRA-BIBLICAL REVELATION: THE CHARISMATIC MOVEMENT

precisely the fact that the charismatic movement rejects *sola Scriptura* by adding extra-biblical sources of revelation next to the Scripture, verified by human experience, that is the cause of the splintering of these churches into such small ecclesiastic bodies.

To some it may seem incredible that the Scriptures rule over our emotions and our experiences. Yet Prov 14:12 states, "There is a way that seems right to a man, but its end is the way of death." Since God created us, he is sovereign over our thoughts, our minds, our heart, our will, our emotions, and our experiences. What we think is good might not be good based on the Bible. Let us examine Luke 16:19–31, the story of Lazarus and the rich man, a well-known parable of Jesus. In it we read about how the rich man lived carefree in opulence, yet Lazarus was a poor and sick man. After both of them died, Lazarus went to heaven to be with Abraham, yet the rich man, not having given thanks to God and repented despite the lavish way God had treated him on earth, was suffering in hell, suffering indescribable pains in the flames. The interesting part, vv. 27–31, reads as follows:

> Then he said, "I beg you therefore, father, that you would send him to my father's house, for I have five brothers, that he may testify to them, lest they also come to this place of torment." Abraham said to him, "They have Moses and the prophets; let them hear them." And he said, "No, father Abraham; *but if one goes to them from the dead, they will repent.*" But he said to him, "*If they do not hear Moses and the prophets, neither will they be persuaded though one rise from the dead.*"

The rich man, in hell, is filled with such an evangelical zeal in that if he himself was unable to escape the torments of hell, he still requests, begs Abraham to send Lazarus back to his kinfolk from the dead, under the impression that if they *experience* such a wondrous miracle as someone coming back from the dead, then they shall surely repent and escape the same fate as his. Yet Abraham answers wisely, following the principle of *sola Scriptura*, saying that experiencing a miracle will not save the rich man's family, but only the Scriptures will save them.[9]

By nature, the charismatic movement is a *gnostic* movement, very much akin to the movement by the same name in the first centuries of the

---

Catholic practice with Protestant practice. If Roman Catholics are honest, they must admit that their church is highly fragmented despite the thin veneer of alleged doctrinal unity.

9. Here the Scripture is referred to as the writings of Moses, the Pentateuch, or the first five books of the Bible. This is the way the Jews sometimes referred to Scriptures.

church after Christ. The gnostics sought secret, hidden knowledge, just as Roman Catholics in their mysteries through spiritual experiences taking place outside of the Bible.

Whereas God gave man the Bible as the exclusive form of divine self-revelation, charismatics and others whom they influence seek a kind of a "backstage entrance God" who speaks directly to them, albeit going past the Bible. However, reaching out to the spiritual realm outside the scope of the Bible does raise concerns. How does a charismatic individual really know that God has spoken to him?

Think of it this way: What if you get a message from the being in the spirit world to go and kill someone or rob a bank? Would you go do it? Obviously, you'd know that the spirit being is not of God if it is telling you to commit an obvious sin. What if the being conveys to you a false doctrine? For example, what if it tells you that all religions are one, or that Jesus didn't rise from the dead? Again, you'd have to question the being, since it obviously contradicts Scripture. But this second case shows you that this kind of extra-biblical information is superfluous since you have the Bible. But there's also a third case: What if the being tells you to do something neutral, or even something seemingly positive? Even with this, there is a problem: we know that the devil comes as an angel of light (2 Cor 11:14) to trick and trap the spiritually curious.

The Bible is the sole *objective* form of religious truth by which we must measure even our own experiences. Just having an experience or hearing words doesn't make the cut—one must validate their subjective experience. After all, any person off the street can claim that they had this or that kind of wonderful experience. In this way some shrewd young men have tried to convince beautiful young women that "God told me that we will get married." The Holy Spirit speaks not just to individuals by themselves but also to the wider church. This underlines the importance of corporate worship. We can verify whether the Holy Spirit did indeed speak to one person if he has spoken to others in the same church about the same issue. The Holy Spirit does not speak to individuals only; he unifies the church.

If you were to challenge a charismatic person as to where he received his revelation, he might come into doubt, especially if he supposedly received word that he can take a paid vacation to the Bahamas for three weeks, something which is definitely not found in the Bible. He might flounder a bit, or he might claim that what he experienced or heard from God can also be found in the Bible.

## EXTRA-BIBLICAL REVELATION: THE CHARISMATIC MOVEMENT

There are two problems that arise here. First, why does it take a dream, or a vision, or a special experience to validate what the Bible says? Christians should be students of God's word, the Bible. These things should stem from a deeper knowledge of God's word. Second, John 10:27 says: "My sheep hear my voice, and I know them, and they follow me." In Acts 17:10–11 we see that the Bereans accepted Paul's teachings, based on his authority. But, since Paul was human, and therefore fallible, the Bereans matched up his teaching with the Bible, to see whether those things taught by Paul were true.

However, when God, the omnipotent, almighty, omniscient Creator, Ruler, and Judge of the entire universe speaks, he certainly can make himself known. Why is it that these charismatics would suddenly doubt God's word when challenged? Perhaps they might have problems with their relationship with God. You can always know God's word simply by immersing yourself in the Scriptures, not in doubtful extra-biblical revelations.

Some charismatics will make the extraordinary claim that following *sola Scriptura*, the Bible itself leads us to believe that there are other valid forms of revelation outside of it. These people claim that *sola Scriptura* implies a denial of itself:

*Sola Scriptura* → *Sola Scriptura* is false

This is a logical fallacy, since it denies the fundamental law of logic, that a statement and its own negative cannot both be true at the same time. Also, according to logic, a false statement never comes from a true statement. If charismatics claim that *sola Scriptura* by its own nature leads to extra-biblical revelation, then obviously, we may now use these extra-biblical sources in theological proofs, traditions, creeds, and whatnot. Clearly, to be consistent, *sola Scriptura* cannot imply itself to be false. No, rather:

*Sola Scriptura* → *Sola Scriptura*

Charismatics may claim that we rely on our own human understanding when using logic. However, we were made in God's image, thus we share God's rational thinking faculties. God himself created the natural world to be subjected to natural laws, described by mathematics. Logic is simply a part of mathematical thinking and is not inherently sinful. Logic is not a human convention. We discover the laws of logic instead of arbitrarily coming up with them on our own. Humans use the laws of logic before even thinking about them.[10]

False prophecies are pandemic in the charismatic movement. Jesus' warning in Matt 24:23–26 rings true:

> Then if anyone says to you, "Look, here is the Christ!" or "There!" do not believe it. For false christs and *false prophets will rise and show great signs and wonders to deceive*, if possible, even the elect. See, I have told you beforehand. Therefore if they say to you, "Look, He is in the desert!" do not go out; or "Look, He is in the inner rooms!" do not believe it.

## An Inordinate Stress on Miracles

As we have seen, the charismatic movement puts an inordinate amount of stress on miracles. Many charismatics believe that if they demonstrate miracles to people, then they will believe. This may seem logical to some, but it is not necessarily theo-logical.

How did Jesus respond to the Pharisees when they desired to see a sign from him? In Matt 12:38–39 we read this: "Then some of the scribes and Pharisees answered, saying, 'Teacher, we want to see a sign from You.' But He answered and said to them, '*An evil and adulterous generation seeks after a sign*, and no sign will be given to it except the sign of the prophet Jonah.'"

Jesus didn't play to the Pharisees' tune. He didn't do as they commanded to satisfy their curiosity. Signs and miracles are quite rare in the Bible. This is because the signs and miracles themselves are not the main "attraction"—Jesus is, the miracle-maker. In the four hundred years before Jesus came to earth there was absolute silence from God, albeit the Jews did have the Scriptures. Jesus himself also did not perform any miracles for thirty years before he began his ministry. John 2:11 says that Jesus began to perform miracles only at the wedding in Cana in Galilee.

Charismatics may respond by saying that Jesus' miracles induced faith in those people that beheld them, but this is not always true. In Luke 17:11–19 only one out of ten healed lepers returned to worship Jesus. In this case, the great majority of the lepers who witnessed the miracle remained in unbelief.

---

10. Geisler and Roach, *Defending Inerrancy*, 264.

## EXTRA-BIBLICAL REVELATION: THE CHARISMATIC MOVEMENT

Jesus says in John 14:12, "Most assuredly, I say to you, he who believes in Me, the works that I do he will do also; *and greater works than these he will do*, because I go to My Father."

Jesus healed the lame, caused the blind to see, and cast out demons. These were all great miracles, but the one thing they all had in common is that they were temporary. People could get sick again, and demons could again possess a person again to make his situation even worse than before (Matt 12:43–45). And of course, except for two examples, all people will die physically—even Lazarus, after Jesus had raised him from the dead.

But what are these works that are greater than those that Jesus did? These greater works involve preaching the gospel so that people will repent from their sins and be born again unto eternal life. You may die, but you cannot lose your salvation. This means that when Christians preach the gospel, and others believe their preaching, then they will live forever and never die.

Sadly, the charismatic movement has missed the mark when it comes to the real miracle and has settled for much, much less.[11] Furthermore, so much seeking out signs and miracles very much de-emphasizes the role that Scripture plays in the lives of charismatics.

### The Scriptures, the Holy Spirit, and Christian Growth

As mentioned previously, the charismatic movement is trichotomist in nature. According to the trichotomist model, man is made up of three components: body, soul, and spirit. This third non-flesh component, the spirit, is in direct contact with God through the Holy Spirit.

Any independent, rational thought is quasi anathema to the charismatic movement and is frowned upon as something that stifles the way in which they think that the Holy Spirit works. In this way, the charismatic movement makes a false accusation against conservative Christians in that they attribute rational, logical thinking about God's word as a sign of humanism and unbelief.

Some within the charismatic movement even go so far as to claim that the Holy Spirit resides only within charismatic circles. They are the "haves," and noncharismatic people are the "have-nots." In other words, noncharismatic Christians are only "half Christians" who have a dry spiritual life and are almost incapable of true spiritual growth.

11. Masters and Whitcomb, *Charismatic Phenomenon*, 22–25.

This mentality on the part of charismatics is wrong, sinful, and judgmental. It also leads to spiritual pride against other Christians. It stems from a misconception of how the Holy Spirit operates and how the Holy Spirit relates to *sola Scriptura*. This way God is put inside a box, since they cannot imagine that the Holy Spirit speaks to and guides Christians in other ways than that in which they think the Holy Spirit operates.

First, if someone does not have the Holy Spirit, that person is not a Christian. Unless a person be born of water and the Spirit, he cannot enter the kingdom of God (John 3:5). One cannot believe in only *two thirds* of God. Think of it this way: if a man says he believes in God the Father and the Holy Spirit, but leaves Jesus Christ, the Son of God, out of the equation, then he has no life in him, since you can be saved only by Jesus Christ, who is the truth, the life, and the way (John 14:6). Thus, if some charismatics claim that the Holy Spirit resides exclusively within their church, this means they are schismatics.

A cult that made similar claims in the early centuries of the church was the cult of Montanus, who claimed that the Holy Spirit was somehow connected to his person. The early church rejected Montanism as a heresy.[12]

The charismatic movement is also similar in a way to Donatism, another heretical movement, which arose in the fourth century and claimed that it was the universal church. The Donatists excluded those people from the church who under duress had denied Jesus during the Roman persecutions. Thus, they made themselves the arbiters of who was authentically Christian, excluding those who had denied the faith.

How does the Bible describe repentance? Let us read Rom 12:1–2:

> I beseech you therefore, brethren, by the mercies of God, that you present your bodies a living sacrifice, holy, acceptable to God, which is your reasonable service. And do not be conformed to this world, but *be transformed by the renewing of your mind*, that you may prove what is that good and acceptable and perfect will of God.

---

12. This way, the charismatic movement resembles the Roman Catholic Church, which claims that the pope is guided by the Holy Spirit when he speaks ex cathedra on questions of faith and morals. In this sense, every charismatic person claims to be his or her own "pope." Besides Arminianism, the charismatic movement also resembles the Roman Catholic Church in its denial of *sola Scriptura* when both espouse dispensationalism, a theology that fragments the word of God into two halves, which will be covered in a following chapter. Small wonder that the Roman Catholic Church has its own charismatic movement!

Here repentance is equated with the renewal of the mind. The Greek word μετάνοια (*metanoia*) refers to a transformational change of mind and heart. It means that the new man thinks differently, and due to his new outlook on life, his acts also follow suit. The new believer thinks and therefore acts differently due to the illumination of the Holy Spirit. One cannot be passive in this process according to charismatic theology. Indeed, to be a consistent charismatic, one would have to be completely passive to the extent that he would have to be as a puppet in God's hands.[13] Of course, charismatics wouldn't say that you should lie around like a vegetable all day long doing nothing, passively waiting for the Holy Spirit to move upon them; this, however, points out the fact that charismatics are inconsistent in their *thinking*.

Man was created in God's image in that God created a brain for Adam with which to think. This is because God himself is a thinking being himself. Thinking and using your mental facilities is not a sin; in fact, it is well pleasing to God. The Psalms tell us over and over again to meditate on God's word (Ps 1:2; 49:3; 77:12; 63:6; 119:78; 143:5). Using our minds to think God's thoughts after him is pleasing to him. God has endowed every believer with certain mental capabilities, and we must then make use of our talents accordingly. Not to do so would be a sin. Whatever is logical may not necessarily be "theo-logical," but this doesn't mean that there is no overlap between man's logic and God's logic. This is an erroneous way of thinking. Faith is not created by reason, but neither is it created without it; reason can be used in both a faithful and a faithless way.[14] See fig. 3.

---

13. Something many Arminian charismatics would likely reject when they incorrectly describe Calvinism's God as being a puppet master.

14. Packer, *Fundamentalism*, 135, 140.

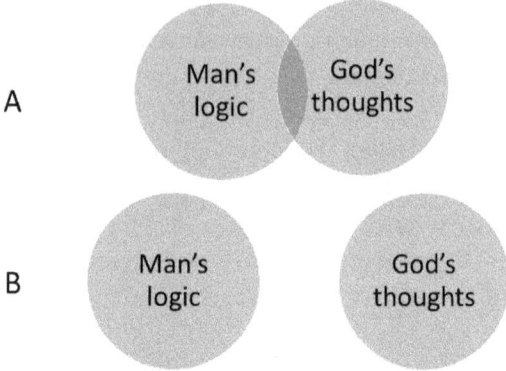

Figure 3. A. Whatever is logical is not necessarily God's way of thinking. However, there is a nonzero overlap between the two. The human mind properly illuminated by the Holy Spirit helps us renew our mind according to God's word. B. The erroneous case in some Pentecostal theologies, where human reason is separated from God's thinking.

In this manner, a godly Christian life does not happen by being "zapped" by the Holy Spirit. It involves listening to the still, small voice of Jesus through the Scriptures (1 Kgs 19:12). Godliness does not happen all at once but is a process. The believer not only talks with God but also walks with God. The work of the Holy Spirit becomes evident in a godly person's life only after some time. The work of the Holy Spirit does not consist of manifesting miracles but rather giving up bad habits, developing new, good ones, and putting on Christ (Rom 13:14; Gal 3:27).

The charismatic movement has a false epistemology, which denies and contradicts *sola Scriptura* and misunderstands the operation of the Holy Spirit. Furthermore, since it also views repentance and sanctification differently, it might well be said that the some in the charismatic movement follow another spirit, foreign to the Scriptures, not the Holy Spirit.

### How Can You Truly Know God's Will?

A big issue in the charismatic controversy is how you can know God's will. You may hear how a charismatic person will tell you that God spoke a word to them. It may sound very spiritual. But is this really the way to discern God's will? Years back I attended a Bible study at a Reformed church that had some charismatic influences. The question under study

# EXTRA-BIBLICAL REVELATION: THE CHARISMATIC MOVEMENT

was how we can know God's will. Since these people were not properly grounded in how to understand *sola Scriptura*, after much debate and discussion back and forth, they arrived at the conclusion that you cannot truly know God's will. This was because they were seeking to know God's will outside the Scripture.

How deflating, isn't it? Isn't God capable of making himself known? Isn't he all-powerful? During the Bible study, they debated questions such as how you can know whom you are going to marry. So many Christians think that must feel some sort of special buzzing feeling, or some electric tension in the air when the two lovers first meet, or that bells and whistles must go off, or some green arrow has to be pointing above the person's head to show who Mr. or Mrs. Right is going to be. But can you really know for sure, is the gnawing question. You can be 99 percent sure. Even 99.9 percent sure. Or even 99.99 percent sure. But not 100 percent sure.

Others make the claim that since it isn't spelled out in the Bible what kind of job I should accept, then I need to somehow get God to supernaturally tell me what to do. And then I can wait for so long inactively, not knowing what to do.

The key here is that *the Bible is enough*. Even more than enough. The Bible contains the will of God. This is because the law of God is one and the same with the will of God. For example, we can know that God wants you to visit the fatherless and widows in their affliction (Jas 1:27), and does not want you to kill, commit adultery, or steal (Exod 20:13–15). God identifies with his word entirely, which is why John 1:1 says the following: "In the beginning was the Word, and the Word was with God, *and the Word was God*." Jesus Christ is the Word, the logos (ὁ λόγος in Greek). If you know Jesus, as revealed by the Scriptures, then you will know God's will, so that "the man of God may be perfect, thoroughly furnished unto all good works" (2 Tim 3:17). Remember that if we add to God's word in the Bible, God will then add to us all the plagues described in that book (Rev 22:18).

Charismatics may claim that they are fully obedient to the will of God in that they don't do anything without "asking God" (by this I mean waiting for a word from God, or a nudge, or something extra-biblical). This sounds very pious and very spiritual. But is it? Does someone with this kind of spirituality fully rely on God 100 percent of the time? If such a person were fully, logically, and thoroughly consistent, that person would be constantly having to stop, turn around, and ask God about his will. What brand of shoes should I buy? What flavor ice cream should I order? You could even take this to the utter extreme. When should I wake up in the morning? Should I put my left or my right leg out of the bed first? *Should I even breathe?!* There were such people who called themselves Christians who searched for God's will in this manner. If these people were consistent, then they would have to realize that they are constantly rebelling against God 99 percent of the day, since they don't inquire of God what bus route they should take to get from one point in the city to the other.

This is why there is Christian freedom as described in the previous paragraph. Christian freedom entails knowing what the Bible says and applying what you know about it to your life situation. Therefore, in such cases when you decide what type of shoes you want to buy, you have freedom in doing so; God gives you the right and responsibility to make your own decision. It's your choice, it's up to you. After all, if someone is free, it doesn't mean that he is a completely mechanical, characterless robot who doesn't have any taste or feelings of his own. Christian freedom is an important teaching, and as such, it will be treated in a later chapter.

## Speaking in Tongues

One of the main characteristics of the charismatic movement is that of allegedly speaking in unknown tongues, otherwise known as γλωσσολαλία in Greek (glossolalia). Speaking in tongues is described in Mark 16; Acts 2, 8, 10, 19; and 1 Cor 12–14. Tongues are used by the charismatic movement as a tool to draw near to God and to experience an exceptionally close relationship with him.

One of the main criticisms of the charismatic movement is what it judges to be the spiritual lifelessness of the mainstream denominations. This was born during a period when lifeless liberalism was widespread. Thus, the charismatic diagnosis is valid when applied to the proper subject. However, its solution is misguided, which is to depart from Scripture as the sole highest authority. The opponent of the charismatic movement is not biblical, conservative, orthodox Christianity but rather lifeless liberalism. Spiritual lifelessness comes from a denial of *sola Scriptura*, not adherence to it.

Therefore, one of the main tenets of the charismatic movement is the return to the spirituality of the early church. Part of this was to reinstitute real Christian spirituality, such as the practice of speaking in tongues, since Jesus Christ is the same yesterday, today, and forever (Heb 13:8). Interestingly, since the charismatic churches are dispensationalist in their thinking, they do not go back far enough into the Old Testament. If they did, they'd have to accept circumcision of infants, which would translate to the baptism of infants today. Following Christ does not necessarily mean imitating him.

Charismatics may charge those who oppose their brand of speaking in tongues with forbidding to speak with tongues (1 Cor 14:29). Speaking in biblical tongues is not being forbidden here, not in the least. However, biblical tongues have ceased (1 Cor 13:8). Therefore, what the charismatic movement practices is not biblical tongues, but rather a counterfeit of true biblical tongues.

## Tongues Are a Sign

Two main issues regarding speaking in tongues are what its purpose was and whether tongues are still valid today. We must understand that the book of Acts was a *descriptive* history of the acts of the apostles after the resurrection of Christ. It is not *proscriptive* as to what the church should be like throughout all of history.[15] First Corinthians 14:22 says the following: "Therefore tongues are for a sign, *not to those who believe but to unbelievers*; but prophesying is not for unbelievers but for those who believe." This is very important here. Speaking in tongues was to serve as a witness to nonbelievers, who did not *yet* have the Scriptures, whereas prophecy was for the church, since the church *had* the Scriptures, and since prophecy is nothing more than explaining and applying the Scriptures to a given issue or question of actual relevance. Numbers 11:29 says, "Then Moses said to him, 'Are you zealous for my sake? Oh, that all the Lord's people were prophets *and* that the Lord would put His Spirit upon them!'"

In Mark 2:1–12 we read about how Jesus healed the man with palsy. In v. 5 he first told the sick man that his sins were forgiven. However, the scribes took offense and accused Jesus of blasphemy, making himself one with God. Jesus had the perfect right to do so because he was one with the Father. To validate his claim thereof, he then told the sick man to rise and take his bed and go home, which he immediately did (vv. 11–12). Jesus verified his identity as the Son of God with his miracles. *Furthermore, the miracles were not the focus of his ministry, but rather his ministry of forgiveness and reconciliation to the Father*: "For the Son of Man has come to seek and to save that which was lost" (Luke 19:10).

15. MacArthur, *Charismatics*, 102–3.

In a similar vein, the miracles that the apostles performed in the book of Acts, such as speaking in tongues, were for a sign that they had authority in spreading the gospel and laying down the foundation of the church. Once the foundation was laid, tongues had no more use, apostolic teaching was finished, and the canon was closed once the Bible had been compiled. There are no more ongoing revelations today. We have only the Bible, and the Bible is enough.

According to 1 Cor 12:28, tongues are actually the least of all spiritual gifts, appearing last in the list of gifts and church offices: "And God has appointed these in the church: first apostles, second prophets, third teachers, after that miracles, then gifts of healings, helps, administrations, *varieties of tongues.*" Indeed, as illustrated by the passage that we will now turn to, Paul exhorts his readers that prophecy is superior to tongues.

First Corinthians 14 describes tongues in detail. Let us quote vv. 1–5:

> Pursue love, and desire spiritual gifts, but *especially that you may prophesy.* For he who speaks in a tongue does not speak to men but to God, for no one understands him; however, in the spirit he speaks mysteries. But he who prophesies speaks edification and exhortation and comfort to men. He who speaks in a tongue *edifies himself, but he who prophesies edifies the church.* I wish you all spoke with tongues, but *even more that you prophesied;* for *he who prophesies is greater than he who speaks with tongues, unless indeed he interprets, that the church may receive edification.*

Some charismatics may try to make a case for private individual tongues out of the first half of v. 2: "For he who speaks in a tongue does not speak to men but to God." However, this is contrasted with the context of vv. 1 and 3, which prefers prophecy over tongues. Prophecy, as we know it, is a gift to the church community. Verse 5 says literally that whatever is spoken in tongues must be interpreted so that everybody benefits from it. There is no sense in hiding anything that God may tell you from others. That is why v. 4, which says, "He who speaks in a tongue edifies himself," mentions this in a negative sense.

Charismatics may then refer to 1 Cor 14:14: "For if I pray in a tongue, my spirit prays, but my understanding is unfruitful." Again, we must look to vv. 13 and 15 for context. Verse 13 again affirms "therefore let him who speaks in a tongue pray that he may interpret." Furthermore, vv. 15 and 16 as a conclusion sum up the thoughts of the previous verses. "What is the conclusion then? I will pray with the spirit, and *I will also pray with the understanding*. I will sing with the spirit, and I will also sing with the understanding. Otherwise, if you bless with the spirit, *how will he who occupies the place of the uninformed say 'Amen' at your giving of thanks, since he does not understand what you say?* For you indeed give thanks well, *but the other is not edified*." These two verses highlight the fact that tongues must be used with understanding, so that others can understand and be edified.[16]

Charismatics portray human understanding, the mind, somewhat as a roadblock to the Holy Spirit, when it is precisely the other way around. The Holy Spirit is a person, illuminating the understanding of the believer to understand and follow his ways.

Tongues are also not special gifts to the individual believer. Many charismatics believe that God has given them a special, individual tongue, which they use in private prayer. This reflects the individualistic nature of charismatic thought. God also deals with his church in a *corporate* manner. This is why the previous passage puts great emphasis on the fact that tongues must be interpreted so that *the whole church can be edified*: "But the manifestation of the Spirit is given to each one for the profit of all" (1 Cor 12:7).

God can even use tongues uttered by a foreign people to chasten his own people.[17] This happened in Isa 28:11–12, where God sent the Assyrians to punish his people for their sins:

> For with stammering lips and another tongue He will speak to this people, to whom He said, "This is the rest with which you may cause the weary to rest," And, "This is the refreshing"; yet they would not hear.

## Tongues Have Ceased

At a certain time point between the first century AD and the second coming of Christ, tongues shall cease. Indeed, it is likely that tongues have long ceased, ever since the early centuries of the church. First Corinthians 13:8–10 speaks about this in the following way:

> Love never fails. But whether there are prophecies, they will fail; whether there are tongues, they will cease; whether there is knowledge, it will vanish away. For we know in part and we prophesy in

---

16. See Masters and Whitcomb, *Charismatic Phenomenon*, 49–51.
17. Burdick, *Tongues*, 29.

part. But when that which is perfect has come, then that which is in part will be done away.

This verse talks about three things: prophecies, tongues, and knowledge. All three will be done with eventually, sooner or later. In the Greek, v. 8 reads: "Ἡ ἀγάπη οὐδέποτε πίπτει. εἴτε δὲ προφητεῖαι, καταργηθήσονται· εἴτε γλῶσσαι, παύσονται· εἴτε γνῶσις, καταργηθήσεται" (*He agape oudepote piptei, eite de profeteiai, katagethesontai, eite glossai, pausontai, eite gnosis, katagethesontai*). Here those that are in part (knowledge and prophecy) are denoted with the verb καταργέω, which means to render entirely useless, abolish, cease, vanish away. Tongues are distinguished from both knowledge and prophecy, in that they are denoted by a separate verb, παύω, which means to restrain, quit, desist, come to an end.

Verse 9 states that both knowledge and prophecy are "in part." Of tongues, it doesn't say this. When the perfect comes, then those that are partial in nature (specifically, knowledge and prophecy) shall disappear, when the perfect comes, whom we shall see face to face, that is, Jesus. From this we know that since tongues are not partial, their time of disappearance will not take place at the second coming, but sometime earlier. This can be seen in fig. 4.

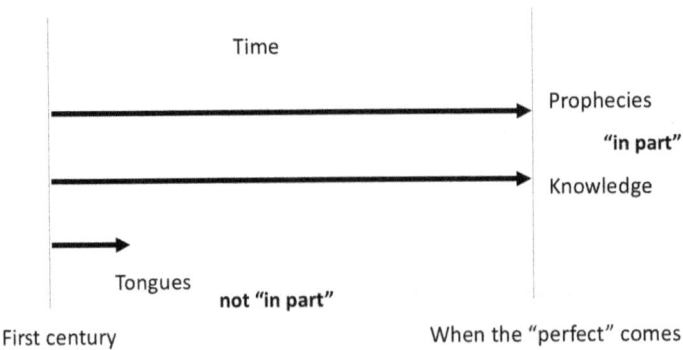

Figure 4. First Corinthians 13:8–10. We prophecy and know in part, and these things shall pass at the second coming of Christ. But tongues, which are not "in part," are done away with earlier.

By applying the Bible to history, we can see that tongues disappeared sometime during the first century AD. Speaking in tongues is mentioned only in the earlier letters of the church fathers. The early church theologians such as Justin Martyr, Augustine, Clement, and Chrysostom spoke about tongues as something already in the past.[18]

For example, Chrysostom wrote this about 1 Cor 12 in his "Twenty-Ninth Homily on the First Epistle of Paul the Apostle to the Corinthians": "This whole place is very obscure: but the obscurity is produced by our ignorance of the facts referred to and by their cessation, being such as then used to occur, but now no longer take place." Augustine said that tongues "were signs adapted to the times," and "that thing was done for a betokening, and it passed away."[19]

By the Middle Ages, tongues were certainly extinct. In modern times there has been no account of any missionary in foreign lands speaking the language of the natives without learning it through many years of effort.[20]

Verse 8 says that knowledge shall vanish away, meaning that the acquisition of all new revealed knowledge shall stop.[21] Jude 3 says, "Beloved, while I was very diligent to write to you concerning our common salvation, I found it necessary to write to you exhorting you to contend earnestly *for the faith which was once for all delivered to the saints.*" According to John 14:26: "But the Helper, the Holy Spirit, whom the Father will send in My name, He will teach you all things, and *bring to your remembrance all things that I said to you.*" Jesus himself says that the role of the Holy Spirit is to remind his followers of everything that he has said to them, not to continuously reveal new information to them in the future.

This means that tongues will have ceased even before this time. These things will happen when the perfect comes. Jesus Christ is the perfect one. But how is it then that Jesus is identified with his revelatory word? Very simple. In John 1:1 Jesus is called the λόγος (logos), or the Word. Jesus is God revealed to us in the flesh. Jesus spoke God's word to us, and the fact that revelation is complete means that God's word is perfect and does not need to be augmented in the last days with any kind of extra-biblical revelation. The Scriptures are enough: "All Scripture is given by inspiration of God, and is profitable for doctrine, for reproof, for correction, for instruction in righteousness, that the man of God may be complete, thoroughly equipped for every good work" (2 Tim 3:16–17).[22] Here Paul is talk-

---

18. MacArthur, *Charismatics*, 163–71.
19. Burdick, *Tongues*, 33–34.
20. Kildahl, *Speaking in Tongues*, 14–17.
21. Robertson, *Final Word*, 68.
22. MacArthur, *Strange Fire*, 224.

ing about all aspects of a believer's life, and the central, all-encompassing, authoritative role the Scriptures play in it.

The charismatic movement claims that there were several groups who practiced prophesy, such as the Montanists from the second to ninth centuries, the Cevenol priests in the late seventeenth century, the Jansenists and the Shakers in the eighteenth century, the Irvingites in the nineteenth century. However, these groups were considered heretical because they uttered false prophecies. Moreover, the Irvingites were Roman Catholics, which would mean that the charismatic movement recognizes the Roman Catholic Church as a legitimate church, even though Rome preaches a works-based gospel.

The Montanist heresy was named after the heretic Montanus, who claimed to be a lyre of the Holy Spirit, allowing the Spirit to make prophetic utterances through his voice. Montanus had two prophetesses, Priscilla and Maximilla. What is interesting is that Maximilla declared the imminent return of Jesus Christ, and that she herself was the last of the prophets. After her, there was no Montanist prophecy for twenty years. The Montanists were condemned by Eusebius of Caesarea and Hippolytus.[23] Clearly, this way the charismatic movement cannot claim that they have historical continuity with either this movement or the apostles.

It was only in the year 1901 when the so-called Kansas City prophets started uttering things in foreign tongues.[24] However, Rev 3:7 says: "These things says He who is holy, He who is true, He who has the key of David, He who opens and no one shuts, and shuts and no one opens." If tongues have ceased, then it is active rebellion against the will of God to restart something that he has caused to cease. Also, if a group within the church claims certain teachings never held to by the early church, then it is almost certain that teaching is heresy, and the movement itself also is in error.

Even Pentecostal authors themselves admit that glossolalia was very sparse all throughout church history. Harris Kaasa writes this in "A Symposium on Speaking in Tongues":

> In summary we may say that there is considerable evidence for the recurrence of this phenomenon. At the same time, no one can fail to be struck by its relative infrequency and by the fact that it occurs mostly among members of (in context) radical sects. Its

---

23. McGoldrick, *Heirs of the Reformation*, 10–12.
24. MacArthur, *Strange Fire*, 170–71.

exceptional presence should not blind us to its general absence in the main stream of church history.[25]

Remember that the Bible was written *for us*, not *to us*, and that imitation is not always the same as following Christ. Certain ordinances come and go throughout salvation history, and tongues were one such thing, a sign of a major salvific event happening as a part of God's plan of salvation, not to continue well into the church age.

What I have described is called the *cessationist* view of the gifts of the Spirit. The contrary view, called *continuationism*, claims that tongues, prophecy, and special healings still exist today. As such, all Pentecostals and charismatics belong to this camp. The cessationist view does not say that all gifts have ceased. For example, miracles may still occur, and people may still be healed; cessationists pray for these things to occur all the time. But these special occurrences are not tied to any one single person with any kind of special anointing. However, visions, prophecies, and dreams have ceased, because these are all processes whereby revelation is increased from God towards man.[26]

## Tongues for All?

Jesus instructed his followers to pray according to Matt 6:9–13. This is the prayer, Our Father, that Jesus spoke in an audible voice; in fact, Jesus never ever prayed in tongues, and if we are to follow his example, then we also should neither pray nor speak in tongues. Jesus also had the Spirit without limitation, and the Spirit came upon him directly at his baptism (Matt 3:16), which was an experience that the apostle Peter described as an anointing with the Holy Spirit and power (Acts 10:38).[27]

Yet another problem with speaking in tongues is that it is very subjective. Anyone can start chattering away in gibberish and call it speaking in tongues. In fact, liberal theologians, Roman Catholics,[28] Mormons, Muslims, Buddhists, Hindus, Shintoists, hippies, and many pagan and occult groups also speak in ecstatic tongues. People have also broken out in ecstatic tongues who suffer from disassociation, epilepsy, hysteria, and

---

25. Burdick, *Tongues*, 34.
26. Buice, "Misunderstanding Cessationism."
27. Burdick, *Tongues*, 13.
28. Andrews, *Spirit Has Come*, 26.

schizophrenia.[29] If all these people can speak in tongues, does it mean that they all have the Spirit of God? Obviously not. It could only mean that speaking in tongues is meaningless because tongues have ceased.

Linguists have also examined the utterances produced by people who allegedly speak in tongues. According to their analysis, the linguistic structure of such utterances is overly simple, and cannot be compared to the more complex structure of real language. For example, no human language has less than five vowel forms, yet charismatic utterances have no more than two to three such vowel forms.[30] Consonant sounds are also restricted, and only a few syllables recur many times in various orders. The intonation of these charismatic tongues sounds completely like American English. Language structure is also missing.[31] It seems that charismatic tongue speakers are trying to speak a new, unknown tongue on the fly but are not very creative at it.

A further problem with modern charismatic tongues is the fact that the tongues that were spoken in Acts 2:5–12 were real, cognate languages. Verses 9–11 go on to list fifteen nations whose languages were being spoken to the visitors to Jerusalem. If someone speaks in tongues, they need to identify the concrete language that they were speaking. In the overwhelming majority of cases, this is not done.

The charismatic movement misses the real meaning of Pentecost. Pentecost is all about the inauguration of the church. It is the first stage of the last days. Previously, in the Old Testament, the church was restricted to the nation of Israel. Now the church includes both Jews and gentiles. God pours out his Spirit on all flesh, upon all nations. That is why God supernaturally moves upon his servants from Galilee to preach the gospel to the visitors to Jerusalem in their own language.

This phenomenon is the reverse of what happened at Babel. At Babel God divided the languages of mankind to hinder them from unifying in idolatrous worship. In Jerusalem at Pentecost God breaks down linguistic barriers so that the gospel may go forth to all nations. The breaking down of barriers can further be seen in Acts 2:17–18, where both sons and daughters shall prophesy. Previously only baby boys were included in the covenant via circumcision; now girls can also partake in baptism. Similarly, both young and old inclusively shall see visions and dream dreams.

---

29. Masters and Whitcomb, *Charismatic Phenomenon*, 32–33.
30. Marston, *Voice of Authority*, 50–51.
31. Burdick, *Tongues*, 61–65.

## EXTRA-BIBLICAL REVELATION: THE CHARISMATIC MOVEMENT

What about the angelic tongues mentioned in 1 Cor 13:1? Are angelic tongues real? Verse 2 asks the rhetorical question about whether one can have all knowledge or know all mysteries or have all faith. Only God has all knowledge and knows all mysteries. These are examples of hyperbole. Thus, the tongues of angels are also hyperbole, an exaggeration. Besides, who knows what angelic tongues are like? Furthermore, angels have only one tongue since today's languages are a result of the division of languages at Babel. This division was a result of man's sin, trying to make himself autonomous from God. Angels are sinless and were not affected by the linguistic event at Babel. Furthermore, since tongues were meant to edify humans (i.e., spread the gospel), it would be pointless to speak in angelic tongues.

The charismatic movement runs into further trouble in vv. 11–13 of 1 Cor 12:

> But *one and the same Spirit* works all these things, distributing to each one individually as He wills. For as the body is one and has many members, but all the members of that one body, being many, are one body, so also *is* Christ. For *by one Spirit* we were all baptized into one body—whether Jews or Greeks, whether slaves or free—and have all been made to drink *into one Spirit*.

These verses declare that the church has the one and the same Spirit, the Holy Spirit. This is the Holy Spirit, who gives gifts to the believers as he wills. This creates a problem for charismatic theology, since speaking in tongues is practiced virtually only in the charismatic churches. Yet the Spirit gives his gifts (tongues, visions) to whomsoever he will, indiscriminately.[32] It would not make sense that believers in noncharismatic churches would not start praying or speaking in tongues. Charismatics would then be forced to say that only charismatic churches are true Christian churches and that all other churches are lifeless, heretical, or have strayed from the faith, and do know not God.

This is uncharitable, since by saying so, charismatics would be adding speaking in tongues as a necessity for salvation. After all, one must not have to speak in tongues to be saved. One has but to trust in the Lord Jesus Christ for his salvation. First Corinthians 12:3 says, "Therefore I make known to you that no one speaking by the Spirit of God calls Jesus accursed, and no one can say that Jesus is Lord except by the Holy Spirit."

We are back to our original problem: if speaking in tongues is real, then people should also be speaking in tongues in noncharismatic

---

32. Andrews, *Spirit Has Come*, 60.

churches. After all, "no good thing will He withhold from those who walk uprightly" (Ps 84:11). But they are not. The solution is that modern speaking in tongues is a false phenomenon, and that it has already ceased, as 1 Cor 13:8 says. Since the charismatic movement is alone in speaking in tongues as it claims, we must therefore conclude that modern speaking in tongues is a false phenomenon.

Moreover, let us examine the way in which Christian prayer occurs. Romans 8:26–27 says: "Likewise the Spirit also helps in our weaknesses. *For we do not know what we should pray for as we ought, but the Spirit Himself makes intercession for us with groanings which cannot be uttered.* Now He who searches the hearts knows what the mind of the Spirit *is*, because He makes intercession for the saints according to *the will of* God." This verse refers to our inability to express the deep spiritual desires of our heart. Therefore, the Holy Spirit needs to intercede for us in ways beyond our understanding and capability to pray.[33]

### Visions and Other Extra-Biblical Revelation

Charismatic people will sometimes describe vivid visions that they have had about certain things that came true in their lives. The way they describe it would convince you that they were really in communication with the Almighty Creator God of the universe. The temptation is very strong to believe that this really is a valid way of communication with God.

Let me describe to you a series of visions a barber who seemed to be charismatic told me while he was cutting my hair. This man had two girls. He claimed that he had a first vision when he saw a girl, about two years old, standing upright with her back towards him, with big, bushy, black, curly hair. Later, his wife found that she was six months pregnant with a baby girl, even though they were convinced that the wife could not bear another child. The girl was born, and when she grew up, she had the same kind of black, bushy, curly hair that the man had seen in his vision.

After hearing such a story, one would be tempted to believe that you would be able to channel God for similar types of visions to get special, personalized information, albeit outside the Bible. But the question remains, is it truly valid?

Again, let us recall 2 Tim 3:16–17: "All Scripture is given by inspiration of God, and is *profitable* for doctrine, for reproof, for correction,

---

33. Burdick, *Tongues*, 25.

## EXTRA-BIBLICAL REVELATION: THE CHARISMATIC MOVEMENT

for instruction in righteousness, that the man of God may be *complete*, thoroughly equipped for every good work." Here the word "profitable" in Greek is ὠφέλιμος (*ofelimos*), which can also be translated as useful, beneficial, advantageous. Its use is to make the man of God perfect, to be able to do all good works. Such a man is whole and lacks nothing. For this task the Scripture is enough. We do not need any other tool, such as visions or oral tradition.

Charismatics may refer to a prophecy in the book of Joel that refers to the people of God seeing visions and dreaming dreams:

> And it shall come to pass afterward that I will pour out My Spirit on all flesh; your sons and your daughters shall prophesy, your old men shall dream dreams, your young men shall see visions. And also on My menservants and on My maidservants I will pour out My Spirit in those days. (Joel 2:28–29)

They claim that this prophecy will occur in the very last days of human history, the modern age, with the advent of the charismatic movement itself. At that time, they claim, Christians will prophesy, dream dreams, and see visions, all of which the charismatic movement wishes to reproduce. However, this is an incorrect interpretation of the text.

Virtually all charismatics are dispensationalists, meaning that they believe that the last days correspond to an era of time in the very distant future. This view is incorrect, because Rev 1:1 (in the very first verse) claims that Jesus Christ will reveal things to his servants, which must come to pass shortly. Not after two thousand years. This verse from the book of Joel clearly refers to the day of Pentecost, since v. 29 says that God will pour out his Spirit in those days, according to Acts 2:33. Surely Christianity did not "start up again" with the charismatic movement. Joel 2:32 also says that in those days the people will call upon the name of the Lord and shall be saved. Surely the charismatic movement is not alone with the gospel, alone with the Holy Spirit.

By listening to such charismatic accounts, one would be tempted to leave the verified path of the Scriptures to chase after visions and dreams. The Scriptures contain enough information to guide us into all truth by the Holy Spirit (John 16:13). Indeed, a friend of mine at church told me how he had visited a charismatic church one Sunday. There was lots of clapping and singing. Then the pastor asked the congregation whoever would like to hear what the Bible says, they should raise their hand. My friend was the only one who raised his hand.

Such charismatic visions really sound like the person who had them truly experienced a miracle. It sounds big, but consider the fact that the Scriptures themselves are the biggest miracle of revelation that a person can ever behold. The martyr Stephen describes the law of God as having been delivered to the Jews by the disposition of angels (Acts 7:53). The Bible is truly miraculous in its origin. It describes events experienced by many thousands of people happening on three continents, written by many different authors with different personalities, who sometimes did not know about some of the other authors, in different literary genre, over a period of approximately four thousand years, from Adam at creation to the apostle John at the close of the first century AD. It describes a series of events in a unified message, all interlocking with each other from the Old to the New Testament, describing how God became man to save sinful men. All this came together for us, containing infallible knowledge, into the divine book called the Bible. Why should we be content with scraps of dubious, subjective revelation, such as singular visions, when we can examine the infallible Scriptures all day long? Reading and understanding the Bible is truly a miracle!

The account of the seemingly charismatic hair stylist goes on. He had a set of two visions when he was undergoing a twelve-and-a-half-hour-long surgery when he claimed he had physically died on two separate occasions and the doctors had thankfully succeeded in resuscitating him both times. The man related that the first time he was biologically dead for a minute and a half. During this time, he described how he was walking in a canyon, wearing the armor of God, the helmet of salvation, the breastplate of righteousness, and the sandals of peace. He was attacked by three large birds with long beaks, which poked a hole into his breastplate. He heard God speaking to him from above. He raised his hand and put it into God's hand, after which he came back to life.

It is questionable as to how these large birds could defeat the breastplate of righteousness, which was given to him supposedly by God. Was he justified at that time? If so, then no large birds or any fiend of hell should be able to break God's righteousness, extrinsically given to us by God himself, unless it was his own self-righteousness. Nevertheless, it seems that the man may have been converted by reaching up his hand to God, who took hold of him and brought him back. On the other hand, this contradicts the doctrine of election, whereby Christ chooses us and not the other way around (John 15:16).

## EXTRA-BIBLICAL REVELATION: THE CHARISMATIC MOVEMENT

The story takes another twist when the man described his second, subsequent biological death during the long operation. The second time he described being in a long tunnel. He could hear singing as he moved along in the tunnel. However, the tunnel got warmer and warmer, hotter and hotter, so hot that he started screaming in pain, realizing that he had landed in hell, *despite his having supposedly been saved during his first experience*. This goes against the biblical teaching that a man cannot lose his salvation, if he has been regenerated by God. God, who hates divorce (Mal 2:16) and who has accepted his people, the church, to be his bride (Rev 21:9), would never ever go against his nature and divorce her. Upon close examination, the wonder-filled stories of charismatics tend to contradict themselves.

Two of the most spectacular out-of-body experiences known in the media today involve a three-year-old boy who allegedly went to heaven and a man who allegedly went to hell for twenty-three minutes.

The first one involves Colton Burpo, who supposedly went to heaven while having an appendectomy. He claims to have met Jesus, who was riding a rainbow-colored horse, and that he sat in Jesus' lap, while angels sang songs to him.[34] The story has sold ten million books and became a "best drama" movie.[35]

The man who went to hell (Bill Wiese) claims that while he became a Christian in 1970, he had an out-of-body experience in 1998, during which he went to hell and spent twenty-three minutes in a cell with two huge demons who brutalized him. He also allegedly met Jesus, who said to him that he must tell people that hell is a real place. However, despite Jesus' command, he only wrote a book about his experience eight years later, in 2006. Again, it is impossible for a Christian to go to hell, since "neither death nor life, nor angels nor principalities nor powers, nor things present nor things to come, nor height nor depth, nor any other created thing, shall be able to separate us from the love of God which is in Christ Jesus our Lord" (Rom 8:38–39). So, either the vision was false or Bill Wiese is not a Christian. The first must be true, the second possibly.[36]

These kinds of visions and supposed out-of-body experiences are misleading at best, and always contain one or more elements of falsehood that contradict the Bible. For example, in the case of Bill Wiese, demons do not have dominion in hell (only God does), meaning that they do not torment

---

34. Osman, *Selling the Stairway to Heaven*, 62.
35. B. Smith, "Heaven Is for Real."
36. Wiese, "23 Minutes in Hell."

people there; that is an element from paganism. According to Rev 20:14, death and Hades themselves are cast into the lake of fire forever, because the devil and his demons themselves must suffer for their iniquities.

Today visions are not the way God communicates to men. In Heb 1:1–2 we read: "God, who at various times and in various ways spoke in time past to the fathers by the prophets, has in these last days spoken to us by His Son, whom He has appointed heir of all things, through whom also He made the worlds."

In Luke 16:19–31 we read about Lazarus and the rich man. Lazarus, poor and needy, goes to Abraham's bosom when he dies, but the rich man goes to hell for neglecting his neighbor. Suffering in hell, the rich man begs Abraham to let Lazarus come back to life and tell his family to repent and do justice. However, Abraham responds by telling the rich man that if his family doesn't listen to Moses or the prophets (the written word), then neither will someone resurrected from the dead persuade them. We learn about hell primarily from the Scriptures and from Jesus, who spoke much about hell. Jesus' word is enough; we don't need a modern-day prophecy to persuade us about this.

That is why it is important that when you hear stories about supernatural experiences from charismatic people you ask them thoroughly about each detail. The details will either contradict one another or the Bible. This is a proper application of the principle of *sola Scriptura*.

One other thing that such stories highlight is the fact that there indeed exists a spiritual world unseen to our physical eyes. This spiritual world is real, and full of activity. However, the devil is anxious to draw us astray from the word of God and to get us to chase after vain visions and other forms of extra-biblical revelation.

Besides all these stories of extraordinary visions, charismatics may refer to 2 Cor 12:1–4:

> It is doubtless not profitable for me to boast. I will come to visions and revelations of the Lord: I know a man in Christ who fourteen years ago—whether in the body I do not know, or whether out of the body I do not know, God knows—such a one was caught up to the third heaven. And I know such a man—whether in the body or out of the body I do not know, God knows—how he was caught up into Paradise and heard inexpressible words, which it is not lawful for a man to utter.

## EXTRA-BIBLICAL REVELATION: THE CHARISMATIC MOVEMENT

This is an example of a vision, even possibly an out-of-body experience, moreover, where a man was caught up to the third heaven, that is, beyond the sky, outer space, and even to heaven itself, and heard wonderful things.

Sounds like a first-century version of Colton Burpo, right? If such an experience could happen to one man, then it could happen to another, correct?

However, the text clearly states that this revelation was meant specifically for this one man. Moreover, it was not allowed for this man to repeat what he heard to others. Why? One can only speculate. It could possibly be that the man's description of heaven to other Christians would have been so wonderful, so attractive, so majestic, that some might even consider committing suicide so that they could cut short their time here on earth and enter this wonderful heaven as soon as possible. But by doing this, they would be sinning against the Lord by killing themselves.

Furthermore, this passage of Scripture comes before the close of the canon, when true miracles and prophecies were still happening. The Bible is also the word of God, sweeter than the honeycomb (Ps 19:10), the book of life (Rev 22:19), and words of life (John 6:68). We should have faith and be content with this and not try to gaze into secrets not meant for us.

### The Bible Is Sufficient

Charismatics do not realize two important things. First, they do not realize that the Bible is sufficient for the Christian faith. They forget that "all Scripture is given by inspiration of God, and is profitable for doctrine, for reproof, for correction, for instruction in righteousness, that the man of God may be complete, thoroughly equipped for every good work" (2 Tim 3:16-17). If you have the Bible, that is enough for a complete, victorious Christian life.

John 20:30-31 says, "And truly Jesus did many other signs in the presence of His disciples, which are not written in this book; but these are written that you may believe that Jesus is the Christ, the Son of God, and that believing you may have life in His name." In other words, Jesus did and said many other things that are not recorded in the Bible. But the Bible itself says that it was given to us so that we may believe. If the charismatic movement keeps pressing its claims to the validity of extra-biblical revelation, it is in the same camp as the Roman Catholic Church.

The reason that the Bible is sufficient for us is because God's word is infinite. The words of Scripture cannot be exhausted in a single reading. They are not mere words of men, but God's words. Thus, they have infinite value. God can always teach us new things through the Scriptures. We can keep coming back to Scripture for it to teach us new things. We should not merely set it aside after reading it through once and then going on to the next thing, the next vision, the next charismatic phenomenon to tickle our ears. By doing so, the charismatic movement detracts from God's infinite character and omnipotent power to be able to do something new. Christians may find new insights in the Bible, but they do not add new doctrines to the Christian faith.[37]

The Bible sets down for us eternal truths, eternal doctrines for us to understand and hold ourselves to. Nobody can ever claim that they fully understand the Scriptures. If so, they are putting themselves on the same level of God. They are saying that since they have finished with Scripture, they do not need it any longer. This is simply wrong.

In other words, since we are finite, and since we do not grasp everything in Scripture, we need to keep coming back to God's infinite wisdom in his word. A drop of water cannot swallow the ocean; rather, it must be dissolved in the ocean itself. It takes humility to remain with God's word.

### Apostles Today?

A major tradition of the charismatic movement is the idea of apostleship in the church. The idea is that since there were apostles in the early church, then this office must still be in existence today since the church must always be the same. But Paul describes how all the apostles personally met Jesus Christ in 1 Cor 15:3–8. In v. 8 he writes: "Then *last of all He was seen by me also,* as by one born out of due time." Here Paul is saying that he was the last apostle. There are no apostles today anymore. Those charismatic preachers who call themselves apostles are in reality false apostles! Furthermore, Luke 16:16 also states that "the law and *the prophets were until John.*" After John there were no new prophets. Thus, there are no new prophets who give us new revelation.

Charismatics may respond by pointing to Eph 4:11, which says, "And He Himself gave some to be apostles, some prophets, some evangelists, and some pastors and teachers." This is written in the New Testament, so some

---

37. Mueller, *Called to Believe*, 17.

may conclude that there are New Testament prophets and apostles. But this is an incorrect view of the church. The vast majority, if not virtually all charismatics are dispensationalists. They do not view Israel as part of the church. Since the church started with Adam in the garden of Eden, it follows that the prophets were given for Old Testament times, and that the apostles were chosen by Christ to build the church, as we shall see shortly.

In this manner, men such as Bob Jones, who is regarded as a great prophet in charismatic circles, are false apostles.[38] The whole idea is simply wrong. Since Eph 2:20 says that the prophets and the apostles are the foundation of the church, these strains of the charismatic movement are in effect attempting to reestablish the church, two thousand years after Christ. It is as if for the charismatic movement that the Holy Spirit was inactive for such a long period of time. This is a wrong view of both the church and the Holy Spirit. If charismatic people follow such men as Bob Jones, they are placing themselves outside of the Christian church and testifying to the fact that they have not the Holy Spirit.

This idea is also wrong, because then we'd have to reinstitute the Old Testament priesthood as well. This would mean going back to animal sacrifice, as though Christ's sacrifice wasn't sufficient. The makeup of the church changes in different periods of salvation history.

Ephesians 2:19–20 says: "Now, therefore, you are no longer strangers and foreigners, but fellow citizens with the saints and members of the household of God, *having been built on the foundation of the apostles and prophets, Jesus Christ Himself being the chief cornerstone.*"

Jesus Christ is building His church, against which the gates of hell cannot prevail (Matt 16:16–18). But the foundation of this church are the apostles and the prophets, holy men of God from both the Old and New Testaments. In Rev 21:12–14 we read that the city of God, the new Jerusalem, has twelve gates, on which the names of the twelve tribes are written. The city also has twelve foundations, which are the twelve apostles of the Lamb.

The foundation of the church has already been laid down. Apostles are no longer needed. If they were needed for further revelation, this would lead to a serious problem. If revelation from God is still ongoing, what if we here today are lacking certain information that is necessary for salvation and which will only come in some future distant time? That would mean that everybody until at least the present moment would be lost. Revelation is complete, and the office of apostle is closed.

---

38. This man is not the same Bob Jones of Bob Jones University.

But what does the word "apostle" really mean? In Greek, the word apostle is derived from the word "to send," ἀποστέλλω. John 13:16 says, "Most assuredly, I say to you, a servant is not greater than his master; *nor is he who is sent greater than he who sent him.*" Jesus Christ himself is an Apostle and High Priest (Heb 3:1). This can make sense, since Jesus sent out his apostles with power, only since he had all power. Ever afterwards this means that the authority and power of an apostle, any man sent by another, can only diminish.

To be a true apostle, one must be personally called by Christ, taught by him for several years, and have seen him alive after his resurrection. Paul fulfills all three criteria in that Jesus called him on the way to Damascus (Acts 9:3–18). Paul was taught by Christ for three years while he was in Arabia (Acts 9:20–25; Gal 1:11–18), which is the same amount of time Jesus spent with the twelve disciples during his earthly ministry.

Charismatics may appeal to Acts 1:23–26, which they describe as the apostolic office being transferred from one man to another. This does not hold, because the election of Matthias to the office of apostle was a special case. Verses 15–21 say that this was done because they had to find a man to take the office of Judas, who betrayed Jesus and committed suicide. Verse 20 says, explicitly, "Let another take his office," as prophesied in the book of Psalms. Furthermore, vv. 21 and 22 lay out another criterion of apostleship that cannot be fulfilled by someone living today. This is notably the criterion that he must have been alive during Jesus' ministry and accompanied the other apostles and must have been a witness to the resurrection of Christ.

Feminist charismatics may appeal to Rom 16:7, which says: "Greet Andronicus and Junia, my countrymen and my fellow prisoners, who are of note among the apostles, who also were in Christ before me." Here we have Junia, Paul's fellow prisoner, who had been in the Lord even before Paul. She, together with Paul and Andronicus, has been suffering for her faith in prison. They are "of note" among the apostles. Does this mean that during Paul's service a female servant had risen to such prominence to be reckoned among the apostles?

The argument is very weak. Ellicott's commentary says that Junia might even be a man's name (alternative spellings being Junias or Junianus).[39] This is the only verse that mentions Junia by name. To make the claim that Junia, a woman, rose to such a rank is purely speculation.

---

39. Ellicott, "Romans 16," v. 7.

We have no way of knowing whether Junia even met Christ by in person to be sent out by him as an apostle, which, as we have seen before, is a criterion of apostleship. Furthermore, the leadership of each church was exclusively male (1 Tim 3:2, 11). The fact that Junia had been noted by the apostles could simply mean that she had done noteworthy service to the apostles, or because of her great faith.

Even if the charismatic argument is correct, Junia would have been the only female apostle, and it seems strange as to why there would be no other female apostles. But even if we made the stretch to accept Junia's female apostleship, this does not mean that women today could be apostles, since the time of the apostles was restricted to the founding of the church.

All in all, the idea of female apostles is new, and has never been seriously endorsed throughout church history.

## Charismatic Traditions

Since the charismatic churches so wholeheartedly admit extra-biblical revelations into the church, it is no wonder that several charismatic traditions have become so widespread in such churches. Even though charismatics are opposed to the authority of any kind of tradition, still, several extra-biblical traditions have been born as the consequence of their thinking. This should not come as a surprise to us, since the way charismatics interpret the Bible is not primarily by using reason and logic, but rather through the method that God speaks to you in every verse; instead of ascertaining what the Bible says, charismatics will read from the Bible what they feel God is trying to tell them. This way charismatics may make up any kind of tradition that pleases them, while trying to pass it off as Scripture based.

The charismatic movement has succumbed heavily to the allure of the world outside the house of God as based on the Scriptures, described in chapter 2, much to their detriment. In the following I will describe some widespread errors and even heresies that occur in the charismatic churches that flow from charismatic tradition.

Another tradition of the charismatic movement is that of women pastors and elders. The charismatic logic is that nothing should restrain the Holy Spirit from speaking through whomever he wants to, let them be men or women.

However, this clearly goes contrary to the word of God, which in 1 Tim 2:12 says, "And I do not permit a woman to teach or to have authority over a man, but to be in silence." Furthermore, 1 Tim 3:2 says, "*A bishop* then must be blameless, *the husband of one wife*, temperate, sober-minded, of good behavior, hospitable, able to teach." Verses 8 and 11 also make it clear that even the deacons should be men and not women. Other verses that say this same thing include Titus 1:5–6: "For this reason I left you in Crete, that you should set in order the things that are lacking, and appoint *elders in every city* as I commanded you—if a man is blameless, *the husband of one wife*, having faithful children not accused of dissipation or insubordination."

Following the charismatic concept of whom the Holy Spirit speaks through, the charismatic movement is very much prone to ecumenism. This is due in part to its very anti-dogmatic stance on teaching as well as to the idea that the Holy Spirit can speak to people despite denominational boundaries, including such bodies as the Roman Catholic Church. This is why neo-Protestant charismatic leaders were willing to pray together with Pope Francis in February 2014. Tony Palmer, an Anglican charismatic, addressed the pope as his "brother bishop." Charismatic leaders have no problem calling the pope their brother in faith, despite deep doctrinal differences between Protestants and Roman Catholics (as we shall see in a later chapter). This can be due only to an unfortunate departure from the principle of *sola Scriptura*.

Since the charismatic movement does not follow the principle of *sola Scriptura*, it is not surprising that the way some charismatics even interpret the Bible follows liberal teaching, as we shall see in the chapter on liberalism. Some charismatics claim that the Bible becomes the living word of God only if we approach it in faith, interacting with the Holy Spirit. Until then the Bible is only a lifeless book. This is nothing less than Barthian liberalism.[40] In essence, those charismatics who hold to such an idea of the interpretation of Scripture are liberals in embryo. This whole idea can simply be refuted by a single verse. Jesus himself says, "The words that I speak unto you, they are spirit, and they are life" (John 6:63). Jesus identifies himself with the word of God since he himself is the *Word* of God (John 1:1). Jesus is the Way, *the Truth*, and the Life (John 14:6).

Yet another strange tradition in the charismatic movement is the existence of so-called snake-handling churches. One hundred twenty-five such churches exist in the Appalachian region in the United States. These churches believe that the so-called "long ending" of the Gospel of Mark in

---

40. Marston, *Voice of Authority*, 31.

16:17–20 is part of the Bible. These verses read in the following way: "And these signs shall follow them that believe; In my name shall they cast out devils; they shall speak with new tongues; *They shall take up serpents; and if they drink any deadly thing, it shall not hurt them*; they shall lay hands on the sick, and they shall recover."

During part of the worship service in these churches the pastor and sometimes other people take out snakes from a container and start handling them, sometimes swinging them around. They do this to prove the validity of Mark 16:17–20, which they claim says that snakes will not harm true believers. This practice started only very recently in 1922 under Pastor George W. Hensley in Cleveland, Tennessee, who started out in the Church of God.

Sadly, many of these charismatic people have been bitten when handling snakes, and some have even died. This testifies to the fact that either Mark 16:17–20 talks about things that are not happening today or that these charismatic people were not true believers. Even more sad is the fact that such charismatic pastors continue snake handling even though their own family members died from snake bites. In one such case in 2018, Pastor Cody Coots of the Full Gospel Tabernacle in Jesus' Name in Middlesboro, Kentucky, was bitten in the face and almost died. Four years previously his own father, Jamie, had died when handling a snake during their church service.[41]

It is true that in Acts 28:3–6 we read about how Paul was bitten by a snake when gathering sticks for a fire on the island of Melita on his way to Rome, but no harm befell him. In this way, Mark 16:17–20 validates this event, which happened shortly after the Gospel of Mark was written. However, such signs and wonders accompanied the apostles only to verify their apostleship. These signs died down even in the first century of the Christian church, even in the lifetime of the apostles. In 2 Cor 12:7 we read that Paul was given a thorn in the flesh so as not to exalt himself beyond all measure.

It is contested as to whether vv. 9–20 really belong to Mark 16. The oldest manuscript copies of Mark, the Codex Sinaiticus and the Codex Vaticanus, do not contain vv. 9–20. These verses are first attested to in the second century. Interestingly, there is a shorter ending to Mark 16 instead of vv. 9–20, which first appears only in the third century: "But they reported briefly to Peter and those with him all that they had been told.

---

41. Truly, "Snake-Handling Pastor Bitten."

And after this, Jesus himself (appeared to them and) sent out by means of them, from east to west, the sacred and imperishable proclamation of eternal salvation" (WSE).

Those who claim that vv. 9–20 are part of Mark's Gospel have to tell us why that ending and not the shorter ending. Any claim that these verses were lost from the original version are only arguments from silence. God preserves his word. Some people may argue that these verses include important parts of Jesus' ascension into heaven and the sending of the apostles. That may be true, but these events are more than made up for in the other Gospels. The Roman Catholic version of the book of Esther contains ten extra verses in chapter 10 and four extra chapters. The rationale for adding these verses and chapters is because the book of Esther doesn't mention the name of the Lord without them. But still, we exclude them from the Bible.

Another extra-biblical error of the charismatic movement is one that claims that Jesus went to hell after he died. Some charismatics further embellish this by saying that Jesus was scourged and beaten by the devil while he was in hell. This is blasphemy and cannot be tolerated in the church. This false heresy is refuted by Luke 23:46, which says, "And when Jesus had cried with a loud voice, he said, Father, *into thy hands I commend my spirit*: and having said thus, he gave up the ghost." Jesus died on the cross, but right after he died, his Spirit went up to the Father. This is because the Prince and Author of life cannot be beaten or conquered by the devil.

By denying *sola Scriptura* charismatic churches thus go so far away from the Scriptures. In such ways they come to deny fundamental teachings of the Bible. For example, the Oneness Pentecostal movement denies the Trinity. They do this by espousing a form of modalism, which says that God was present as the Father until the time of Christ, whereby he then became the Son of God. Now in these last days God is present only as the Holy Spirit. Other charismatic errors claim that God was a failure or deny the atonement.

Following is a list of some charismatic traditions that contradict the Bible. Their biblical refutation is also provided.

1. God's revelation continues today. *Refutation:* "The faith which was once for all delivered to the saints" (Jude 1:3).
2. The Bible is not enough for faith (but also extra-biblical revelation). *Refutation:* "All Scripture is given by inspiration of God, and is profitable for doctrine, for reproof, for correction, for instruction

in righteousness, that the man of God may be complete, thoroughly equipped for every good work" (2 Tim 3:16–17).

3. The Holy Spirit resides only within the Pentecostal movement. *Refutation:* "No one speaking by the Spirit of God calls Jesus accursed, and no one can say that Jesus is Lord except by the Holy Spirit" (1 Cor 12:3).

4. The charismatic person can control when the Holy Spirit speaks. *Refutation:* "The wind blows where it wishes, and you hear the sound of it, but cannot tell where it comes from and where it goes. So is everyone who is born of the Spirit" (John 3:8).

5. There are different levels of association or fullness of the Holy Spirit, leading to different classes of believers. *Refutation:* "Or do you not know that your body is the temple of the Holy Spirit who is in you, whom you have from God, and you are not your own?" (1 Cor 6:19).

6. Tongues are alive today. *Refutation:* "Whether there are tongues, they will cease" (1 Cor 13:8).

7. Believers must pray in tongues. *Refutation:* "In this manner, therefore, pray" (Matt 6:9).

8. Modern tongues are the same today as in the first century in the book of Acts. *Refutation:* "Then there appeared to them divided tongues, as of fire, and one sat upon each of them" (Acts 2:3).

9. Miraculous healings still happen today always. *Refutation:* "And lest I should be exalted above measure by the abundance of the revelations, a thorn in the flesh was given to me, a messenger of Satan to buffet me, lest I be exalted above measure" (2 Cor 12:7).

10. God speaks to the individual charismatic believer. *Refutation:* "If anyone speaks in a tongue, let there be two or at the most three, each in turn, and let one interpret" (1 Cor 14:27).

11. Each charismatic believer receives his own special tongue. *Refutation:* "And how is it that we hear, each in our own language in which we were born?" (Acts 2:8).

12. The greatest gift of God is prophecy. *Refutation:* "And now abide faith, hope, love, these three; *but the greatest of these is love*" (1 Cor 13:13).

13. There are apostles today. *Refutation:* "After that He was seen by James, then by all the apostles. Then last of all He was seen by me also, as by one born out of due time" (1 Cor 15:7–8).

14. You can lose the gift of the Holy Spirit. *Refutation:* "And I will pray the Father, and He will give you another Helper, that He may abide with you forever" (John 14:16).

15. God gives us visions even today. *Refutation:* "God, who at various times and in various ways spoke in time past to the fathers by the prophets, has in these last days spoken to us by His Son" (Heb 1:1–2).

16. A Christian must receive the second blessing. *Refutation:* "Beware lest anyone cheat you through philosophy and empty deceit, according to the tradition of men, according to the basic principles of the world, and not according to Christ. For in Him dwells all the fullness of the Godhead bodily; and you are complete in Him, who is the head of all principality and power" (Col 2:8–10).

17. Women can be pastors. *Refutation:* "A bishop then must be blameless, the husband of one wife" (1 Tim 3:2).

18. The Spirit of Christ is something different than the Holy Spirit, merely a principle imparted to the believer. *Refutation:* "But you are not in the flesh but in the Spirit, if indeed the Spirit of God dwells in you. Now if anyone does not have the Spirit of Christ, he is not His" (Rom 8:9).

19. Even followers of Christ can be demonized. *Refutation:* "Or do you not know that your body is the temple of the Holy Spirit who is in you" (1 Cor 6:19).

20. Believers will experience no hardships in their lives, only blessings. *Refutation:* "These things I have spoken to you, that in Me you may have peace. In the world you will have tribulation" (John 16:33).

## Conclusion

The charismatic movement may claim that it follows *sola Scriptura*, but in reality, it is very far from it. *Sola Scriptura* and the charismatic movement mutually exclude one another. Only one can exist over the other. Since *sola Scriptura* has a basis in the Bible, we must then reject charismatic theology.

In fact, charismatic teachings are so amorphous that it is quite difficult to define what the term "charismatic" means, simply because there are so many groups that may defy certain definitions. Because of its denial of *sola Scriptura*, the charismatic movement cannot be even said to have a proper theological framework. Rather, it is a loose collection of oftentimes contradictory and ever-shifting ideas. Furthermore, since there are so many charismatic churches, with such great variety of error, sin is certain to ensue. As opposed to the Roman Catholic charge that *sola Scriptura* breeds variety, it is precisely breakage from *sola Scriptura* that causes denominational diversity as seen in the charismatic movement.

It is also important to see here that the charismatic movement leads us away from the house of Scripture into the realm of tongues, dreams, and visions, whose times have long passed. These things were signs only in previous stages of church history, and are no longer for today, since today we have the Scriptures. Leading men away from Scripture will surely have negative moral consequences as well. Interestingly, through its denial of *sola Scriptura*, the charismatic movement shares traits with both the Roman Catholic Church and liberalism, as we shall see later.

Beware anyone who would lead you outside the house of Scripture into all sorts of extra-biblical error. "For I testify to everyone who hears the words of the prophecy of this book: If anyone adds to these things, God will add to him the plagues that are written in this book" (Rev 22:18).

# The Erosive Tide of Liberalism

For assuredly, I say to you, till heaven and earth pass away, one jot or one tittle will by no means pass from the law till all is fulfilled.

MATT 5:18

### Introduction

BESIDES ROMAN CATHOLICISM AND the charismatic movement, there is another theological trend that leads to error based on the way it relates to Scripture. This movement is called theological liberalism. Instead of adding to the Scriptures, like Roman Catholicism and the charismatic movement, liberalism takes away from the authority of Scripture. Liberalism claims that only certain parts of Scriptures are authoritative, but its many streams and traditions often contradict one another as to which parts.

In this way, it goes against 2 Tim 3:16–17 and the principle of *tota Scriptura*, which both say that all of Scripture is God-breathed and therefore authoritative. By removing certain verses from Scripture, liberalism sets itself up as the arbiter of what is inspired and what is not, therefore daring to judge God himself.

Besides the myriads of extra-biblical ecclesioles stemming from the charismatic movement, the inherent fallacy of liberalism is evident in that there are multitudes of theological schools of liberalism, each with only one single teaching in common, namely the denial of *sola Scriptura*. Denial of *sola Scriptura* always multiplies error.

In fact, theological liberalism itself started in the eighteenth century as a result of certain philosophical trends represented by such philosophers as Kant and Hegel and the theologian Schleiermacher, which were based on the supreme power of man's intellect. Whereas the charismatic movement measures everything based on human experience, theological liberalism makes *unenlightened* human reason the sole highest authority. Immanuel Kant himself declared that "the pure religion of reason" is the interpretive principle of Scripture.[1] Therefore, if something cannot be explained in the Bible based on science or reason, then that part of the Bible is relegated to mere myth or legend.

Later, during the Romantic movement—still a child of the Enlightenment period due to its rejection of dogmas—instead of cold, hard reason, theologians such as Schleiermacher based theology not on Scripture, but on human experience and emotion (*Gefühl*). They wanted something that humans could verify with their own intellect and feeling.[2] This error is shared by both liberalism and the charismatic movement. Both raise some element of the human psyche above that of Scripture.

With the advent of naturalistic Darwinism, liberalism went a step further. To many, it seemed that Darwinian evolution had proven that the biblical account of Genesis was untenable and therefore untrustworthy. But if the Scriptures were wrong in one place, then they could also be wrong in other places. This highlights the logical inconsistency of theistic evolution, which we will deal with shortly, and which is akin to theological liberalism.

Another tendency of theistic evolution is to turn history and facts into philosophy and ideas. It claims that the historical events in Gen 1–11 are merely ideas, even myths, that never happened. The six days of creation and the fall give way to evolutionary deep time. As such, it detaches the Bible from reality, and endangers the reality of salvation history itself. This is a hallmark of Gnosticism, a competitor of orthodox Christianity.[3]

Theistic evolution reinterprets the book of Genesis in the light of evolutionary theory but does not treat the rest of the Bible the same way. After having thrown a literal creation, the fall into sin, the worldwide flood, and the Babel event out of the Bible, liberalism consistently proceeds to erase the virgin birth of Jesus Christ, the resurrection, and anything and everything that sounds even slightly miraculous in the Bible. Theological liberalism is nothing less than a complete rewrite of the Bible, expunging whole parts of it that are held to be repugnant to scientific naturalism. It is even more than that—liberalism is an attempt by modern theologians to

1. Grenz and Olson, *20th-Century Theology*, 30.
2. Grenz and Olson, *20th-Century Theology*, 42–43.
3. Jordan, *Creation in Six Days*, 71–79.

completely reinvent Christianity in the light of modern evolutionary materialism. As such, it gives the first place to secular ideology instead of to the Scriptures. Liberalism is the archenemy of *sola Scriptura*, and the friend and slave of the world, thus the enemy of God (Jas 4:4).

The theologian Ritschl made a separation between "scientific" and "religious" knowledge, as if the two didn't communicate with one another. Between the two types of knowledge, one will have to win out.[4] Obviously, since liberal theology is the lackey of rationalism, then "scientific" knowledge will win out, negating *sola Scriptura*.

In the twentieth century, Karl Barth would go even further and claim that the Bible is nothing more than human attempts to reproduce the word of God in human words and thoughts and in specific human situations.[5] This makes the human understanding the arbiter above God. God's word can be understood only as far as human understanding can grasp it. This limits God. But God cannot be limited in what he reveals, even if we don't comprehend his mysteries, such as the Trinity. If liberal theology were consistent, it would have to reject the Trinity.

Another liberal theologian, Rudolf Bultmann, carried the damage even further. Not only did he separate so-called scientific knowledge from religious knowledge, but whatever was objectionable to science, he labelled a myth—basically a falsehood. This way Bultmann cut out certain mythical parts of the Bible, a process he called *demythologization*. In this manner Bultmann built upon previous theologians, such as Adolf von Harnack, who said that these mythological elements are like the husk that must be removed to find the kernel of truth inside. In Bultmann's view, the whole New Testament was husk, but instead of removing it, he transformed the Christian message of the New Testament into existentialist Christianity.[6]

For Bultmann, the real historical Jesus was not important. Historical facts were not the focus, but a personal response to Christ in the gospels.[7] This of course begs the question, if one must respond to Christ, how can this be done if Jesus Christ was never real? Doctrines depend upon certain events that happen in salvation history. If the event goes, then so does the meaning that is attached to it.[8] Jesus insists many times in the gospels that

---

4. Grenz and Olson, *20th-Century Theology*, 53.
5. Grenz and Olson, *20th-Century Theology*, 71.
6. Strimple, *Modern Search*, 121.
7. Grenz and Olson, *20th-Century Theology*, 88–90.
8. Machen, *Christianity and Liberalism*, 23–25.

not only is he an example of faith, but also the object of faith (John 4:21; 5:24; 6:35, 40, 47; 7:38; 11:25; 12:44, 46; 14:1, 11–12).[9]

## The "Canon within a Canon"

In their efforts to save what they perceive as the sinking ship of Christianity, liberals have jettisoned various portions of the Bible. Therefore, instead of speaking about the canon of Scripture, which consists of the entire Scripture, from the first Hebrew letter in the Old Testament to the last Greek letter in the New Testament, liberals talk about the phantom "canon within a canon." Based on a given liberal theologian's definition of which part of the Scripture is authoritative and which is not, a core part of the Bible is retained that is deemed to be relevant and authoritative. Liberal theologians have all sorts of rules and reasonings as to which parts of the canon they wish to retain and which ones to ignore. They also contradict one another with their rules.

This goes even further. Theological liberalism claims that the Bible is a dead book, which "comes alive," so to speak, based only on whether the Holy Spirit moves upon the understanding of the believer who is reading the book. This way, theological liberalism wishes to spiritualize the toxic teaching that it imbibes into so many people sitting in the pews in their churches.

In a peculiar way, however, this is somewhat akin to how people in the charismatic and neo-evangelical movements interpret the Scriptures. Interpreting the Scriptures in this way entails trying to find out what the Scripture means "to me." In other words, certain words in the Scripture can mean multiple things, depending on what kind of situation the reader is in at the actual moment. This is nothing less than moral relativism, because in this way one can make the Scriptures say whatever one wants.

It is important to note that the Scriptures were written *for us* and not *to us*. The historical narratives and parables in the Bible were written for us so that we may know who God is, and that we may trust in him. If God helped those heroes of the faith mentioned in the Bible, then so can God also help us.

---

9. Machen, *Christianity and Liberalism*, 72–73.

## Revelation versus Reason

Let us note that despite the fact that biblical Christianity makes much of understanding the Bible (Rom 12:1–2) instead of emotions or experience, it is not the same as theological liberalism. This is important, because at the beginning of this book I defined *sola Scriptura* in that Scripture, *and not our interpretation of it*, is the sole highest authority. Liberalism interprets the Scriptures based on mere human reason and logic and completely leaves out the divine illuminating influence of the Holy Spirit who "will guide you into all truth; for He will not speak on His own authority, but whatever He hears He will speak; and He will tell you things to come" (John 16:13). This way, the charismatic criticism against relying solely on the human intellect when interpreting the Scriptures is valid but should be directed against liberals and not Bible-believing Christians (a sign that charismatics are not truly capable of discerning the Spirit).

In the words of R. L. Dabney, the famous evangelical preacher:

> The Scriptures exercise all that authority which their own intrinsic truth confers; this reason does not confer, but receives. Here, then, is the radical difference between intelligent faith and rationalism. Faith makes reason the recipient of revealed light; rationalism makes it the source. Faith begins by recognizing, on reasonable grounds, the infallibility of the Word, and thenceforward bows to it implicitly.[10]

This is an important concept to understand. John 21:12 says: "Jesus said to them, 'Come and eat breakfast.' Yet none of the disciples dared ask Him, 'Who are You?'—knowing that it was the Lord." This is a similar issue to how we must discern the canon with regards to Roman Catholicism. It is also related to discerning the Holy Spirit regarding the issue of the charismatic movement. With regards to liberal theology, this means that the believer recognizes the work of the Holy Spirit and is gifted with a kind of indescribable assurance and certainty what the word of God is telling him. This is because just as two people walk with each other, they can discern each other's personalities. How much better it is not to leave everything to mere human reason, which is capable of errors, but put all our trust in the Holy Spirit, who "will guide you into all truth; for He will not speak on His own authority, but whatever He hears He will speak; and He will tell you things to come" (John 16:13).

10. Dabney, *Evangelical Eloquence*, 189.

## The Lingering Effects of Karl Barth

Karl Barth, the famous Swiss theologian, along with others, created a school of theology popularly called neoorthodoxy in reaction to the liberalism of his day. However, it turned out to be only a little less liberal than the theology it critiqued. This is because it lacked a proper appreciation for the authority of Scripture. Unfortunately, neoorthodoxy has spread widely within evangelical circles and has influenced many. These include Emil Brunner, G. C. Berkouwer, Jack Bartlett Rogers, Clark Pinnock (a big proponent of open theism), Peter Enns, and others.

According to Barth, a distinction must be made between the word of God and the written pages of Scripture. The reading of the Bible is more in accordance with extracting the meaning of the Bible.[11] Naturally, this way, the Bible can be detoured to read into it anything that the interpreter wishes to read into it.

Copying Barth, many Evangelicals and Pentecostals may say that they prize the words of Jesus even more than the Bible. According to Barth, the Bible can be likened to a scratched record, through which the Master's voice can be heard.[12] Emil Brunner states, "The word of Scripture is not in itself the word of God but of man, just as the historical appearance of the God-man is in itself that of a man."[13] G. C. Berkouwer claims that all human writings err since their authors err. Since the Bible was written by humans, it too contains errors.[14] Indeed, many Evangelicals are following this trend, relying on inner feelings to tell them what is true, rather than the propositional truth of the Bible.[15]

One can easily see the fatal logic of this train of thought. If the Bible errs, then God has erred. This means that God is either deceptive or incompetent. Either way, he is not God. If the Bible is a scratched record, as Barth contends, how can we at all know how many scratches there are on that record, and where? We would know nothing for certain. We could easily mistake falsehood for the Master's voice, and vice versa, we might misinterpret the Master's voice for falsehood. Moreover, many books written by

---

11. Kapic and McCormack, *Mapping Modern Theology*, 81.
12. Geisler and Roach, *Defending Inerrancy*, 286.
13. Geisler and Roach, *Defending Inerrancy*, 310.
14. Geisler and Roach, *Defending Inerrancy*, 310.
15. Schaeffer, *Great Evangelical Disaster*, 51–54.

men are without error. This implies that these fallible men have bested the fallible god of Karl Barth.

Interestingly, Barth's view of the incarnation of Christ was fairly orthodox. One cannot but wonder why he did not draw the logical conclusion that just as Christ, who was God in the flesh, could not err, thus the Bible also is inerrant. Barth should have seen that the Bible is not purely the work of human hands. Rather, it was coauthored by God. Even though men may err, God does not. God preserved the truth in the pages of the Bible from human error.[16]

## Theistic Evolution

Theistic evolution is a theory that God used evolution to create the universe, the earth, and living organisms. This theory basically tries to accommodate both the theory of evolution and the biblical concept of creation. In virtually all its forms, theistic evolution does not regard Gen 1–11 as literal history, but rather as some sort of allegorical description of God as Creator. Historically, theistic evolution is a recent development, starting from the nineteenth century, prompted by Darwin's theory of evolution. It is also a denial of the principle of *sola Scriptura* properly in the liberal sense.

Proponents of theistic evolution will claim that the Bible says nothing about evolution or origins, and that the literalists' claim of such is really a case of *solo Scriptura*. However, several Bible verses contradict the statements of evolutionary theory, and as such we must reject it based on *sola Scriptura*. We will examine such verses that highlight this later.

Furthermore, an appeal by theistic evolutionists to many church fathers and Reformers who allegedly accommodated the science of their day is based on false assumptions. While most church fathers interpreted Genesis literally, many of them added symbolism to the literal backbone of their interpretation.[17] The church fathers and the Reformers were fallen men, and if they break the principle of *sola Scriptura*, their examples should not be followed.

---

16. Geisler and Roach, *Defending Inerrancy*, 314.
17. Tay, "Misrepresenting Creationism," 44.

## Concordance

More exactly, theistic evolution is a form of concordance that claims that there are two or more sources of truth that must be brought into agreement with one another. In this case, this corresponds to the Bible and the scientific theory of a nonbelieving naturalist. The very nature of concordance demands that we accept these multiple sources of truth with the exact same level of authority. Neither can be allowed to be modified, and all statements from all sources must be brought into agreement with one another. In this sense, theistic evolution is akin to the three sources of authority of the Roman Catholic Church.[18]

Concordance is a denial of *sola Scriptura* in that it accepts more than one source of unquestionable authority. It puts God and man on the same level. As described previously, either man's ideas are deified or the Scriptures are brought down to the level of mere human reasoning.

Even both can happen at the same time, as with theistic evolution, where Genesis is relegated to the sphere of mere symbolism and myth, and evolutionary theory is elevated to the level of absolute dogma. It is wishful to think that two sources of authority can be forcefully morphed together. One single contradiction between one statement from one of the sources of authority with another statement from another source of authority being brought into concordance with the first upsets the whole delicate balance between the two. According to Matt 6:24, "No one can serve two masters; for either he will hate the one and love the other, or else he will be loyal to the one and despise the other. You cannot serve God and mammon."

Concordance was popularized in an important book by the Evangelical Bernard Ramm, titled *The Christian View of Science*. The position Ramm holds is that truth must be a conjuncture of both science and religion. According to his view, science is the study of nature, whereas theology is the understanding of God. The speech of God in nature and in Scripture must accord.[19] However, if science and theology do not overlap, then this leads to Gnosticism (the separation of the material world from the spiritual world). God's word does make propositional statements about the real world (miracles, the virgin birth, the resurrection, etc.).

Many professing Christians have slid from an orthodox, literal reading of Genesis not because of doubts that the literal interpretation was correct.

---

18. That is, the Bible, tradition, and church authority.
19. Ramm, *Christian View of Science*, 26–28, 35–36.

Nothing inherent in the text of Scripture itself brought about this change in thought. Rather, it is an external factor, such as man-made theories of origin, that raises doubts in the minds of these people. For example, Karl W. Giberson describes his fall from the orthodox view when he attended Eastern Nazarene College. Multiple arguments from geology and biology convinced Giberson to give up his orthodox views on creation. This is because Giberson did not hold to *sola Scriptura* to hang on to his faith, which was further weakened by his compromising religion teachers.[20]

For example, Giberson asks why Adam would be given such a bland name such as "man," or Eve "woman."[21] This last statement is incorrect, because Eve (*Cheva*) in Hebrew means life, living, or the mother of all living. Interestingly, in our modern day and age, there are actual programming languages that have seemingly bland names. For example, NPL stands for "new programming language," and APL, "a programming language."[22]

The view of Dennis Venema and Scot McKnight from the theistic evolutionist organization BioLogos is that neither the Bible nor science (however vaguely they define it) should dominate one another. Rather there should be a dialogue between the two. Science can help in biblical exegesis, just as the Bible can provide horizons and vistas for scientists.[23] Indeed, Venema and McKnight redefine *sola Scriptura* as *prima Scriptura*. What this means is that Scripture is *the first of many authorities* to consult when thinking about a given question. Other authorities of equal value are various human theories about origins of equal standing, even though they come after the Bible.[24]

Venema himself states that he had been raised to believe a literal six-day, young-earth interpretation of Gen 1 and 2. However, when he studied science, he started questioning this interpretation, and thought that it was well intended, but misguided and in need of rethinking.[25] In his mind, when Genesis and science collided, "science" won out. Venema and McKnight end up divorcing the Bible from scientific reality by assigning the Bible to the ancient Near East and science to the modern West. They talk about scientific facts as though they are set in stone. Yet,

20. Giberson, *Saving Darwin*, 1–15.
21. Giberson, *Saving Darwin*, 8.
22. Sebesta, *Concepts of Programming Languages*, 67, 70.
23. Venema and McKnight, *Adam and the Genome*, 94.
24. Venema and McKnight, *Adam and the Genome*, 105–6.
25. Venema and McKnight, *Adam and the Genome*, 95.

scientific theories come and go, and there are numerous ways to interpret scientific facts (also vaguely defined by these same authors).[26] Creation scientists are not afraid of some interpretations of scientific facts that contradict their faith. If either the Bible or evolutionary theory are going to crumble, it would have to be evolutionary theory. If we accommodate our interpretation of the Bible to actual scientific theories of the day, this means only that truth is mutable and relative.

Venema and McKnight simply think that a man formed from dust, a woman formed from his side, talking snakes, a worldwide flood, a population of eight humans repopulating the earth all seem allegorical. Yet a talking donkey (Num 22:28–30), water turning into wine, fish and bread being multiplied, the dead rising from their graves are perfectly acceptable. Venema and McKnight are inconsistent.

Another example of concordance is Dru Johnson's book *What Hath Darwin to Do with Scripture?* As opposed to many evangelical theistic evolutionists, Johnson is consistent with importing evolutionary ideology into the Bible. Sadly, there can't be two sheriffs in town; one will get his way over the other. There can be only one guiding hermeneutic when interpreting the Bible. Either the Bible interprets itself or we let some other guiding principle take over, in which case we can read anything we want into the Bible.

Johnson ends up reinterpreting Genesis in the light of how he defines resource scarcity, fitness, and generation as parts of evolutionary theory.[27] These completely upend the biblical view of salvation history. Johnson denies scriptural inerrancy, claiming that the biblical authors were inaccurate in some of the things they wrote, and holds Genesis to be a myth.[28] But Johnson's consistency leads him further on to reinterpret the gospel, namely that people must become fit to receive salvation. Those who relax the Torah or do not receive the kingdom like a child are unfit. This is nothing less than works-based righteousness. Finally, since Johnson bases his views on materialism, he ends up calling the virgin birth of Jesus and his resurrection and ascension into heaven a robust fantasy.[29] Such is the outworking of consistent theistic evolutionary theory.

---

26. According to John Ioannidis, most scientific publications have subsequently been shown to be false due to biases, low study power, and false or meaningless relationships in the study ("Most Published Research Findings").
27. Johnson, *What Hath Darwin*, 16.
28. Johnson, *What Hath Darwin*, 16–17.
29. Johnson, *What Hath Darwin*, 190.

Evolution quite obviously contradicts biblical creation in that it is a continuously ongoing materialistic process, without end, yet even many theistic evolutionists must agree that creation is the completed work of God, who rested on the seventh day and hallowed it (Gen 2:3). Furthermore, evolutionary theory states the earth is of old age, yet the genealogies in Genesis, Matthew, and Luke do not add up to more than several thousand years.

Sadly, as in the case of theistic evolution, when we try to bring the Bible into concordance with anything else, the Bible suffers in the process. The word "evolution" is not found anywhere in the Bible but is rather an invention of humans being forced into the Bible. According to 1 Cor 15:37–39,

> And what you sow, you do not sow that body that shall be, but mere grain—perhaps wheat or some other grain. But God gives it a body as He pleases, and to each seed its own body. All flesh is not the same flesh, but there is one kind of flesh of men, another flesh of animals, another of fish, and another of birds.

This verse means that God created each animal according to its kind, separate from one another, which is exactly what is described in Gen 1:24–25. According to evolution, continuity exists between the first cellular life-forms and modern species. Technically, according to evolutionary theory, our great-great-great-... grandparents were bacteria. Therefore, in a sense, all flesh would be the same flesh, even the flesh of plants and animals since all life-forms have a common ancestor.

Most importantly, however, the biblical view of salvation history completely contradicts theistic evolution. According to the evolutionary worldview, death precedes man in the form of natural selection. According to evolution, death is a natural process, culling the weaker members of the species until a newer species evolves and supplants the weaker species. However, according to the Bible, death is a consequence of man's sin: "And the Lord God commanded the man, saying, 'Of every tree of the garden thou mayest freely eat: but of the tree of the knowledge of good and evil you shall not eat, for in the day that you eat of it you shall surely die.'" (Gen 2:16–17). When Adam ate of the fruit of the tree of the knowledge of good and evil, he died spiritually. However, since man's spirit is tied to his body, spiritual death is tied to physical death, because as God said at Adam's fall, "dust thou art, and unto dust shalt thou return" (Gen 3:19).

According to evolutionary theory, sin is not a part of the natural world; sin does not even exist. As such, Christ's selfless atonement for sin on the cross is completely meaningless. As such, evolution and the gospel completely contradict one another. Evolution is all about survival of the fittest and beating the competition. Christianity is all about love, selflessness, self-denial. The Bible says that if a man loses his life for Christ's sake, he shall find it (Matt 16:25). Christ taught us that if a man strikes you on your right cheek, turn to him the other also; if a man takes away your coat, give him your cloak as well; if a man makes you go one mile, go another with him (Matt 5:39–41). The height and pinnacle of self-denial culminated in Christ's sacrifice for the sin of the world on the cross. Love conquers selfishness. Creation is vindicated over evolution. *Sola Scriptura* is true.

Evolution also denies the authority of Scriptura in another major way. This involves the actual inspiration and compilation of the Scriptures. Liberal theology uses evolutionary theory as a tool to explain the origin of the Bible itself. Liberal theology starts out from evolution as an overarching theory that stands above even the Bible itself.

Characteristically, since liberal theology is compromised when it comes to the Genesis account of origins, it ignores the account or downplays its significance. For example, W. H. Bellinger and many other liberal theologians deny the role of physical death on Gen 2–3.[30] As such, liberal theology is an ideology different from biblical, evangelical Christianity.

According to evolution, humankind is constantly evolving physically, but also mentally and spiritually. According to C. H. Dodd, "The life of the spirit of man, is evolutionary in the sense that its movements and changes are continuous and organic."[31] As such, man's understandings of divine truths are also constantly changing. This is why liberal theology interprets Gen 1–11 as a myth. God's truth evolves along with man's understanding of it. What was true for primitive cultures tens of thousands of years ago may not be true now for modern man. In complete contradiction to *sola Scriptura*, Dodd writes that there is no final court of appeal beyond the religious intuition of mankind. Furthermore, God discloses his revelation in the facts of history, as they are experienced by man. Such men include those who are open to their impact and are qualified to understand them, such as the half-mythical Abraham, the legendary Moses, or the prophet Micaiah.[32]

---

30. Bellinger, *Introducing Old Testament Theology*, 72–73.
31. Dodd, *Authority of the Bible*, 227.
32. Dodd, *Authority of the Bible*, 230.

The question raises itself, what special breed of men is qualified to understand the revelation of God in the facts of history? This statement appears to be a reversion to the priestly caste of Roman Catholicism. In stark contrast, Jesus tells us in Matt 18:2, "Assuredly, I say to you, unless you are converted and become as little children, you will by no means enter the kingdom of heaven."

In more extreme versions of theistic evolution, as espoused by the liberal Jesuit Pierre Teilhard de Chardin, even God himself is subjected to the process of evolutionary development. God will be present in his supreme, sovereign form only at the end of all time.

This form of theistic evolution blatantly violates *sola Scriptura*, which holds to the eternal truths of Scripture and also denies the Trinity. Jesus says in Matt 5:18, "Assuredly, I say to you, till heaven and earth pass away, one jot or one tittle will by no means pass from the law till all is fulfilled." The gospel is not different for people in ancient times as for people in modern times. Jesus Christ is the same yesterday, today, and forever (Heb 13:8).

## What Is Science All About?

Many atheists and theistic evolutionists do not clearly define what science and religion are all about. Since theistic evolutionists think that science has proven the earth to be billions of years old and that the fossil evidence shows that humans evolved all the way from single-celled organisms, then the early chapters of evidence cannot be taken literally.

But what is science? Atheists treat science as though it must be pursued to the complete exclusion of God and that religion has no authority to dictate to science. But is this really true? Ramm briefly describes science as all knowledge.[33] In this, he is correct, and it is a pity that he did not develop this line of thought any further.

If science is defined simply as all knowledge, then the acquisition of knowledge can be defined in many different ways by various philosophies of science. Scientific naturalism is only one way of acquiring knowledge, whereas intelligent design is another. Atheists may wish to eliminate theology as a science, but this would also mean putting psychology, sociology, history, anthropology, and geology beyond the pale of science. After all,

---

33. Ramm, *Christian View of Science*, 34.

observation, repetition, and testing are all three basic hallmarks of science, but which do not apply to evolution.

It is only the atheist's sleight of hand to state that since science studies nature, there is nature only. This is a logical fallacy. Atheists have no right to make metaphysical, religious claims about the supernatural, when their microscopes are focused on the natural world.

Science did not begin with Darwin, but rather was birthed in the wider circle of medieval Christian Europe in the early universities, such as the ones at Oxford, Paris, and Bologna. We can name any number of well-known Christian scientists who laid down the base of modern science, including Euler, Pascal, Newton, Pasteur, Boyle, etc. The science of taxonomy, established by Carl Linnaeus, was based on the idea that species were created by God.

Creation science, for example, studies the handiwork of God, not the hand of God. The intelligent design movement seeks to find clues in the natural world that point to an intelligent source, just like how linguists could decipher the Rosetta Stone, since they knew it was written by other humans. Or we could also mention the search for extraterrestrial intelligence (SETI) programs that try to contact alien intelligence based on certain criteria such as detecting signals representing a series of prime numbers.

Theories of origins cannot be reduced to the monolithic theory of evolution. Science thrives best when there are multiple views on the market, as opposed to a single monopoly. Beware of one hand clapping, the saying goes. Around Darwin's time, for example, so-called natural theologians grouped different organisms together based on various criteria, which they thought corresponded to the kinds mentioned in Gen 1 (vv. 10–11, 21). This theory survived until the modern day in the scientific field of study known as *baraminology*.[34] This means that there are viable alternatives to evolutionary theory, and we do not need to compromise with atheistic philosophy.

## Genesis Is Not the Product of Ancient Near East Mythologies

Since liberal theology rejects the slightest suggestion that the creation account in Genesis must be taken literally, they fall back on the heathen

---

34. *Baraminology* is the study of the created kinds in Gen 1. The name is made up of two Hebrew words. *Bara* means "God created," and *min* means "kind," "group," or "type." An example of a kind is cats. Cats breed with cats but not with dogs, which is another kind. Kinds represent mutually exclusive reproductive communities.

suggestion that Genesis is a myth, a product of the mythologies of the ancient Near East. Many liberal theologians claim that Genesis was based off a creation myth formulated in Babylon and was incorporated into the Bible during the Babylonian captivity of the Jews.

Such a suggestion does complete violence to the text of Genesis and the principle of *sola Scriptura*. According to such views, Genesis is merely the product of human culture, and not God's revelation to man. It portrays God as someone who is weak and totally unoriginal and leaves it up to man to find out for himself how things originated. Furthermore, this is a kind of concordance that elevates pagan mythologies to the same level of God's word. This way, Scripture is no longer the sole highest authority, but is forced to make way for pagan myths.

It acquiescently allows a pagan culture to dictate to the people of God what to believe, instead of God telling us how he created everything. Even worse, such an idea is a total cave-in to the atheist suggestion that the Bible is purely a myth, and has no basis in reality, and can therefore be laid aside.

Genesis is not the mere copycat product of ancient Near Eastern mythologies. According to Egyptian mythology, the god Atum was a primordial mold, from which all life arose. This is sheer pantheism. In another version of Egyptian cosmology from the twenty-first dynasty, death is hailed as the creator of gods and men, a god in the form of a winged snake with legs.[35] Far from being original, this mirrors the biblical concept of the snake originally having legs in Gen 3:14. Also, according to Canaanite mythology, the supreme god, El, is enthroned at the sources of the two rivers in the deeps of the water.

Babylonian mythology says that the earth is made up of six flat plates, tied to one another by a series of cables. A hallmark of the Babylonian origin myth, described in the Enuma Elish, is the concept of multiple gods warring with each other, until one god slays the other. This concept flies directly in the face of the biblical view of origins. It suggests that God and Satan are on equal footing with each other, and that God must struggle with Satan to kill him. This contradicts the goodness of creation: if God created everything good (Gen 1:31), then this excludes God creating an evil being such as Satan.

Greek mythology says that the universe is made up of successive spheres, according to Ptolemy. This false view was subsequently incorporated into medieval cosmology but is unbiblical. These ancient Near East

---

35. Klingbeil, *Genesis Creation Account*, 28.

mythologies have nothing to do with the Genesis account of creation, which describes a three-tiered creation made up of sky, earth, and waters.[36]

## "Biblical" Theology

In neo-evangelical circles a form of liberal theology has survived. It may adhere to truly evangelical doctrines, such as the virgin birth or the resurrection, but its methods still go back to the old liberal theology. "Biblical theology" may even condemn the old liberalism, but it is going the same path as what it condemns. These tools include textual criticism, the use of reason, and the appeal to authority. As such, even though modern Evangelicals may profess true doctrine, the liberal undertow may lead them away from the Bible. Since this form of liberalism is not overt, it is that much more insidious.[37]

For example, this is why theistic evolution is widespread in many evangelical churches. In this "biblical" theology, different authorities in science, psychology, history, culture, etc. are called upon to impart knowledge.[38] This, however, implies that there are some neutral facts outside of God, meaning that neither is God Almighty nor is the Scripture authoritative over all things. "Biblical" theology wants to be biblical, and it may appeal to the Bible, but it is not fully biblical, because it still uses the critical methods of the old liberalism.

One such critical method employed by "biblical" theology is the historical-critical method, used by the German theological liberal Ernst Troeltsch. According to this method, historical criticism can achieve only probability, not certainty—this, instead of the sure testimony of the Holy Spirit (John 16:13). It also uses a form of uniformitarianism, stating that if we don't see miracles today, then miracles never happened, even in the past. Last, a closed continuum of cause and effect implies a lack of outside intervention.[39]

The fundamental error of the "biblical theology" movement is that it doesn't realize that all facts are oriented towards God's truth. Like bricks

---

36. Klingbeil, *Genesis Creation Account*, 11–16.
37. Packer, *Fundamentalism*, 153–60.
38. For example, this is why some Christians will seek counseling help from secular psychologists, when the church pastor should be competently trained in administering biblical counseling from God's word. Remember, God's word is enough to make the man of God complete, thoroughly equipped for all good works (2 Tim 3:16–17).
39. Allert, *Early Christian Readings*, 97–100.

in a wall, or threads in a tapestry, or brushstrokes in a painting, when all facts are put together and interpreted properly, they all speak about one unit, one whole, which is God's truth.

## The End Result of Liberal Theology

In the long run, however, liberalism itself is inconsistent in its very essence. We can compare liberalism to a man in the middle of the water in a sinking boat with a hole in it. Water is coming into the boat, completely flooding it. Instead of trying to shovel the water out of the boat, the boatman is throwing the boat's cargo overboard to save the boat. Similarly, liberal theologians are throwing out one part of the Bible after the other to make it more palatable to atheists and secularists. In this manner, the church becomes more and more like the world, which is the exact opposite of what it was called to do. Sam Harris rightly calls out liberal theologians in their error by saying that if one part of the Bible is in error, then you can throw it all out.[40] Liberals are very inconsistent.[41] It is sad to see that secularists like Sam Harris understand the issue better than supposedly learned men who have been put in charge of souls.

Indeed, despite this, some liberal pastors and theologians go the full measure and end up as atheists. Figure 5 epitomizes this terrible slide into unbelief very well. In 2003, a Lutheran pastor, Thorkild Grosbøll, in Denmark, came out admitting that he was an atheist.[42] Notably, the liberal theologian Paul Tillich said, "God does not exist. He is being—itself beyond essence and existence. Therefore, to argue that God exists is to deny him." He denied the Trinity and the resurrection, and claimed that the Bible was not the word of God. Proponents of the "Christian atheism" movement in the 1960s claimed Tillich as their mentor. Another liberal theologian had such audacity as to draw a cartoon of Jesus Christ wearing an inner tube, implying that Jesus never performed any miracles, such as walking on water.

With a liberal theology comes liberal morals. The liberal churches are the ones that accept gay marriage and abortion openheartedly. Two very well-known liberal theologians, Karl Barth and Paul Tillich, an ecumenicist, led sexually immoral lifestyles. Some female pastors of these liberal

---

40. Harris, *Letter to Christian Nation*.
41. Packer, *Fundamentalism*, 163.
42. Mohler, "Something Rotten in Denmark."

churches even go so far as to bless abortion clinics.[43] These churches are fast losing members and are ever shrinking in size. For example, the United Church of Christ dropped from 2.2 million members in 1957 to 773,000 members in 2021 (65 percent) and declined from 8,283 congregations in 1957 to 4,794 in 2018 (42 percent).[44]

Figure 5. The descent into unbelief begins by denying *sola Scriptura*.

Some people in the true church believe that the liberal church will die away by itself. This may or may not be true because the depravity of men's hearts requires that God should say only things that would tickle their ears and rest their conscience, instead of accusing them of their sin. This old type of liberalism has faded away, but liberalism persists, albeit in a different format. Its expression may be different, but its tools are the same. This new form of liberalism is called "biblical" theology, which exists in neo-evangelical circles, but is unbiblical in its character. "There is nothing new under the sun" (Eccl 1:9).

43. Zauzmer, "Clergy Gather to Bless."
44. G. Smith, "UCC Membership Decline."

# Roman Catholicism: Man Supplements God's Word

> He said to them, "All too well you reject the commandment of God, that you may keep your tradition."
>
> MARK 7:9

### Introduction

THE CHARISMATIC MOVEMENT MAY ignore *sola Scriptura*, though some may pay lip service to it. Liberalism erodes it to accommodate modernist ideas. But compared to these ideologies, Roman Catholicism attacks it with all its vigor. The fight for *sola Scriptura* is the most intense when dealing with Roman Catholicism. Rome knows all too well that a very large number of its doctrines cannot be found in Scripture. Therefore, Rome has created an elaborate argument to make room for some of her extra-biblical traditions, to uphold them.

### Revelation According to Rome

According to the *Catechism of the Catholic Church*, "In keeping with the Lord's command, the Gospel was handed on in two ways:

> —*Orally* by the apostles who handed on, by the spoken word of their preaching, by the example they gave, by the institutions they established, what they themselves had received—whether from the lips of Christ, from his way of life and his works, or whether they had learned it at the prompting of the Holy Spirit

> —*In writing* by those apostles and other men associated with the apostles who, under the inspiration of the same Holy Spirit, committed the message of salvation to writing.[1]

Furthermore, the Roman Catholic Church claims that she alone possesses apostolic authority to explain the Scriptures, since she was the church that was founded by Jesus in Matt 16:18. According to Rome, we receive divine revelation through three channels: the Holy Scriptures, tradition, and the teaching authority of the church. Together, according to Roman Catholic imagery, these three sources of revelation form a three-legged stool. Because it has three legs, the legs form a stabilized plane, so therefore the stool cannot fall over. The three-legged stool is compared to a stool of a single leg, which consists of Scripture alone, which Romanism claims to be unstable.

This imagery is inaccurate. Scripture can stand alone by itself. God's word can support itself, just as the ark of God could in 2 Sam 6:6–7. As we have seen in a previous chapter, the Bible is self-authenticating. The idea that we must support God's truth with our own traditions is wrong. God's word in the Bible is sufficient and does not need to be supported by human opinion, just as it is unnecessary to mix evolutionary theory with the book of Genesis, as we have seen in previous chapters.

Rome claims to have a high view of Scripture, in that she believes that all words of Scripture are breathed by God. However, at the same time, Rome has a low view of Scripture, if she thinks that Scripture must be augmented by human tradition.

Roman Catholic apologetes require that Protestants provide Bible verses that support *sola Scriptura*. This is a subtle yet erroneous argument. It presupposes that tradition is already valid, and that one must justify reducing God's word to Scripture only. As discussed previously, both Protestants and Roman Catholics both accept the divine authority of Scripture. However, Roman Catholics add their own tradition to the Scriptures. Thus, it is Roman Catholics who must give a reason as to why they are adding to the primary source of divine revelation, which is the Bible. From the outset it is the Roman Catholics who must be on the defense, not the Protestants.

Let us take a look at some Bible verses that explicitly support *sola Scriptura*, and which show that the tradition of the Roman Catholic Church is unnecessary, and cannot, and should not ever be placed on the same level as the Bible.

---

1. Interdicasterial Commission, *Catechism of Catholic Church*, para. 76.

The first is Heb 1:1–2: "God, who at various times and *in various ways spoke in time past* to the fathers by the prophets, has in these last days *spoken to us by His Son*, whom He has appointed heir of all things, through whom also He made the worlds." Here the writer of Hebrews is comparing the way God revealed himself to his people in the Old Testament times as well as in the New Testament times. In the Old Testament, as to a church under age, God spoke via the mouth of his prophets, via dreams, visions, and the like. That is, God used multiple channels in speaking to his people. God even used signs, such as in Judg 6:37, when Gideon put out a piece of wool, which was wet the next morning, with the earth being dry underneath it, then by this he knew that God would favor him in battle.

In New Testament times God has spoken to us only by his Son, Jesus Christ, alone. This is only one singular source, not multiple ones. Jesus Christ is the Word, the λόγος (logos). Jesus Christ equated himself with the Word.

Some may argue that if *sola Scriptura* is a principle found in the Bible, then it must be true for all time, not just in New Testament times. However, this is not true, as Heb 1:1–2 itself divides human history into two segments, namely in times past and in these last days. In times past, multiple channels of divine revelation existed, since the Scriptures had not yet been written. But now, since we have the Scriptures, they are sufficient for us in all things. Now we have only one form of revelation, despite it not necessarily being valid for all epochs of history.

Table 2. The various source(s) of revelation in the Protestant and the Roman Catholic model

|                    | Scripture | Tradition | Church Authority |
| ------------------ | --------- | --------- | ---------------- |
| Protestantism      | √         | X         | X                |
| Roman Catholicism  | √         | √         | √                |

We can further illuminate this by asking a question that John Calvin asked in the *Institutes* about the nature of divine revelation: What is pure divine revelation? What is a pure source? A pure source of information is such that every bit of information that it contains stands as an authority by itself. In other words, it doesn't need to be verified, but is *self-authenticating*. Jesus says: "My sheep hear my voice, and I know them, and they follow Me" (John 10:27).

For more clarity, let us look at the table below:

Table 3. Which authority is self-authenticating?

| Scripture | Tradition | Church Authority |
|---|---|---|
| √ | X | X |

In our case, the Bible doesn't need to be verified, simply because all of it is the word of God. As 2 Tim 3:16 says, all Scripture is given by inspiration of God. Francis Schaeffer writes that "finite man in the external universe, being finite, has no sufficient reference point if he begins absolutely and autonomously from himself; thus he needs *certain knowledge*. God gives us this in the Scripture."[2]

Church tradition, we know, is not self-authenticating, since it is merely the opinion of men about Scripture. Man's interpretation of God's word and God's word itself are not on the same level just as we are not on the same level as God. Tradition is human in origin as opposed to the Scriptures, which are the word of God. Church authority is also of human origin, and it is well known that the early theologians contradicted one another and even themselves. Origen was known to have taken multiple views on many different doctrines. Though the early theologians may have been wise men, they really are only fallible interpreters of Scripture. Why interpret fallible interpreters, thereby possibly increasing error, when we can interpret the Scriptures ourselves?

Table 4. Which source is divine in origin?

| Scripture | Tradition | Church Authority |
|---|---|---|
| √ | X | X |

When pressed, Roman Catholics will admit that one cannot put the opinions of men on the same level as Scripture. This shows that even the greatest opponents of *sola Scriptura* admit at a visceral level that the Scriptures are the highest source of divine knowledge. This also indicates that many Roman Catholics mistake the teaching of *solo Scriptura* with

---

2. Schaeffer, *God Who Is There*, 120; emphasis added.

that of *sola Scriptura*. There is a single-letter difference here, but it makes worlds of difference.

## Is Oral Tradition Valid?

Rome uses another argument by which to validate her tradition. The claim is that not everything that Jesus preached and taught was written down. In other words, there are certain things that Jesus said that are kept alive in memory and handed down by oral tradition, in a word-of-mouth format. Roman Catholics cite 2 Thess 2:15 to support the idea of divine revelation being passed on in an oral fashion: "Therefore, brethren, stand fast and hold the *traditions* which you were taught, whether *by word* or our epistle."

This argument sounds plausible on the face of it, but when we look at it in more detail, the logic breaks down. The question we need to ask is, is the type of tradition that Paul writes about in Second Thessalonians the same type of tradition that the Roman Catholic Church claims as her own? This is important because there are many kinds of tradition. The Jews had their own traditions, which Jesus condemned (Mark 7:9). Different people groups also keep alive traditions that were started at some point during their history. Is Roman Catholic oral tradition valid?

Let us turn to the early theologian and historian Eusebius, who could arguably be a source of tradition himself. In his book *The History of the Church*, which encompasses the first three hundred years of church history, Eusebius writes this about the oral tradition of the apostle Peter after the time of Christ:

> So brightly shone the light of true religion on the minds of Peter's hearers that, not satisfied with a single hearing or with the oral teaching of the divine message, they resorted to appeals of every kind to induce Mark (whose gospel we have) as he was a follower of Peter, to leave them in writing a summary of the instructions they had received by word of mouth, nor did they let him go till they had persuaded him and thus became responsible for the writing of what is known as the Gospel according to Mark.[3]

Thus, we see that the kind of tradition that Paul is writing about in 2 Thess 2 is not what Rome is talking about. A true definition of tradition is that tradition is the same thing as Scripture. In other words, *Scripture is the written form of*

---

3. Eusebius, *History of the Church*, 64.

## ROMAN CATHOLICISM: MAN SUPPLEMENTS GOD'S WORD

*tradition*. Think about it: Would it make sense for the apostles to randomly leave out certain important doctrines from the Scripture (papacy, Mariology, purgatory), and leave others in? Why leave such important oral tradition to the winds of forgetfulness? To exclude important teachings from being written down is simply unwise. Was the apostle Peter selectively putting the divine teaching of Jesus Christ into two different boxes (see fig. 6)?

| Scripture | Tradition |
|---|---|
| Creation | The Papacy |
| The Trinity | Mary and the Saints |
| The Virgin Birth | Transubstantiation |
| The Resurrection | Prayers to the Dead |
| The Atonement | Church Hierarchy |

Figure 6. Roman Catholic teaching sorts different doctrines into two separate boxes, arbitrarily. Those doctrines that are distinctly Roman Catholic are not found in the Bible.

Furthermore, since Eusebius wrote a history of the early church, it would be interesting to see whether he mentions anything about Roman Catholic tradition. This is important, because the first three hundred years of Christian history is an important time, following the time of Christ, encompassing the preaching of the apostles, and serving as a conduit to our modern day and age.

Eusebius mentions only two things that can in any measure have anything to do with Roman Catholic theology: he mentions the bishop's miter and the fact that the theologian Origen (AD 184–253) held to the idea that the church was founded on the apostle Peter. However, the Jewish priests also wore a miter of a very different shape than that worn by Roman Catholic clergy. Furthermore, Origen's view on Peter being the rock is only one of many possible interpretations of Matt 16:18, and does not establish apostolic succession, which is necessary for the doctrine of the papacy. This is because in Matt 18:18 the self-same authority given to Peter is given to the other apostles as well.

## Church Authority and the Early Theologians

Rome's argument is that even though the Bible has divine authority, the best way to interpret it is to listen to the early theologians of the church, such as Clement, Irenaeus, or Chrysostom, who lived in the closest proximity to the time of Jesus and his apostles. Not that these early theologians were actual apostles ordained by Christ, though. In this sense Rome is banking on the idea that these early theologians got their facts right and correctly understood what Jesus said. However, according to Rom 3:4, "Let God be true, but every man a liar." This brings us back to one of our original main points. We know for sure that the Bible is divine, yet the opinion of man is tainted. In this manner the early theologians, wise as they were by the grace of God, are playing only *second fiddle* to the word of God. Yet Rome puts so much stock in these second fiddlers.

Rome forgets an important thing, namely that *the words of these men themselves must also be interpreted and understood, no differently than the words of Jesus Christ in the Bible.* The words of Jesus can and have been misunderstood throughout history. But this is also true of the words of these early theologians. Thus, we arrive at an important question: Whose words would you rather misinterpret? The pure words of the Son of God or the impure words of fallen men? This is an important distinction: though we know Jesus' words are all true, despite our misunderstanding them, we cannot know if the words of the early theologians are true or not, *whether we interpret them correctly or not.*

Rome claims that her teaching is the standard of truth, and that she has the fullness of faith. If that is true, then one would think that in the early centuries after Jesus ascended into heaven, the church would have been in complete unity. However, the Bible tells us that this is not the case. Early in the church, divisions arose among the first believers (Rom 16:17; 1 Cor 1:10). Furthermore, the apostle Paul forewarns the church at Ephesus that grievous wolves will enter the church, not sparing the flock (Acts 20:29). In Rev 2:20 they even suffer the false prophetess Jezebel to seduce God's servants to commit fornication and eat things sacrificed unto idols.

Therefore, to be able to separate true doctrine from false doctrine, to tell a false teacher from one who speaks the truth, we must apply a higher authority, one higher than the mortal sinners who make up the church. This infallible divine source of revelation can be only the Bible. This way the Bible stands alone above the teaching authority of any church. The human authority of the church can be only relative to the absolute divine authority of the Bible. Whatever a man says can have authority only if it comports with the true meaning of Scripture. This is why the Bible alone, *and not any man's opinion of it*, is the sole highest authority.

In effect, the Roman Catholic Church is just like any other Protestant church when it comes to her authority. We cannot just simply take Rome's word for granted that she correctly interprets Matt 16:16–18 to mean that Jesus established the Roman Catholic Church as his church. This is a circular argument. It would simply be begging the question of from where Rome derives her authority.

Rome may claim that even though many theologians in the early centuries had differing opinions, in later times their opinions were distilled to form a solid unit of teaching. This cannot be true, since today one billion Catholics still form varying factions within and outside the Roman Catholic Church, such as the liberal Jesuits, the conservative Jesuits, the Sedevacantists, the Old Catholic Church, the Latin Rite Catholics, the charismatics, and the so-called cafeteria Catholics who pick and choose from their own church's teachings, some of whom even support abortion and homosexuality, not the least of whom is Pope Francis himself.[4]

Today we have a pope who says that homosexuality is acceptable and that atheists can go to heaven. Large numbers of people who hold to the same idea doesn't necessarily mean that they are right. Numbers don't necessarily translate to correct doctrine. Otherwise, we would have to follow Islam since it also has over one billion adherents. Jesus tells us in Matt 7:13, "Enter by the narrow gate; for wide is the gate and broad is the way that leads to destruction, and there are many who go in by it."

As in a previous chapter on the charismatic movement, it would be useful to mention a few examples to illustrate the fact that contrary to her opinion, the Roman Catholic Church is lacking in the fullness of faith.

The most important one is how we view forgiveness and salvation. We must be sure not to take a one-sided view of things. God forgives sinners once and forever as a judge. This is called *judicial forgiveness*. If you are forgiven judicially, then Christ's righteousness covers your sins, and you are saved forever. However, it is also important that once a believer has a living relationship with God the Father, he must continuously confess his sins and be forgiven by his Father. This is called *paternal forgiveness* and is akin to family members making up to one another. Both types of forgiveness are

---

4. Lawler, *Lost Shepherd*.

essential to the Christian walk. The following table illustrates the relationship of judicial and paternal forgiveness:[5]

Table 5. Comparison between judicial and paternal forgiveness

| Judicial Forgiveness | Paternal Forgiveness |
| --- | --- |
| Given by God as our Judge (Heb 12:23) | Given by God as our Father (Luke 11:2–4) |
| Based on the sacrifice of Jesus (Rom 3:24) | Based on the sacrifice of Jesus (1 John 1:7–9) |
| Not repeated (Ps 103:12) | Repeated (1 John 1:9–10) |
| Not achieved by animal sacrifices (Heb 10:4) | Achieved by animal sacrifices (Lev. 5:5; 1 John 1:9) |
| Appropriated by faith (Gen 15:6; Rom 5:1) | Appropriated by confession (Lev 5:5; 16:21) |
| Brings us into fellowship with God (Rom 5:1–2) | Restores us to fellowship with God (1 John 1:3–9) |
| Keeps us from being separated from God in hell (Rev 20:11–15) | Keeps us from being separated from God on earth (Ps 66:18) |
| Related to justification (being declared righteous) | Related to sanctification (being made righteous) |

Rome neglects judicial forgiveness, and therefore many Roman Catholics fear that if they die with any unconfessed sins, they will go to hell. This is not true. God the Father would never let his cherished and beloved children die in sin, and willfully throw them into hellfire if he had worked so hard to save them in the first place.

At the same time, paternal forgiveness is also an important part of the picture complementing judicial forgiveness. Just because someone has repented, it doesn't mean they can sin all they want. Jesus did tell the sinful woman caught in adultery that he did not judge her but to go *and sin no more* (John 8:11). Sanctification is the flip side and application of salvation.

---

5. This material was produced by Dr. Sidney Dyer of Greenville Presbyterian Theological Seminary for his course on the Gospels and Acts.

Though Christians sin, they are forgiven by judicial forgiveness, but there is still a wall between God and them and others. Sin divides and makes us grow cold towards God. It is not right, and therefore we must always remember to repent and confess our sins before God. The Bible is full of verses that stress both types of forgiveness.

Roman Catholics and antinomians stress one set of verses over against the other. That is why it is rather the Reformed religion that has the fullness of faith: "Just as He chose us in Him before the foundation of the world, that we should be holy and without blame before Him in love, having predestined us to adoption as sons by Jesus Christ to Himself, according to the good pleasure of His will" (Eph 1:4–5).

Let us look at a couple of more examples where Rome contradicts the Bible. Rome withholds the cup from the laity during her Mass, due to alleged health issues.[6] Canon 1 of the twenty-first session of Trent declares: "If any one saith, that, by the precept of God, or, by necessity of salvation, all and each of the faithful of Christ ought to receive both species of the most holy sacrament not consecrating; let him be anathema."

Sadly, this declaration places the Lord Jesus Christ under anathema, who declared that both bread and wine be served during the supper: "Then He took the cup, and gave thanks, and gave it to them, saying, '*Drink from it, all of you.* For this is My blood of the new covenant, which is shed for many for the remission of sins'" (Matt 26:27–28).

A meal is never complete without food and drink.

Next, the Council of Trent demands that her priests all be celibate. This was a tradition started by Pope Gregory VII in response to the rampant sexual immorality among the priesthood in the eleventh century in the church. However, it contradicts the explicit command laid down in 1 Tim 3:2: "*A bishop then must be blameless, the husband of one wife*, temperate, sober-minded, of good behavior, hospitable, able to teach."

## Acts 17:10–11 and Church Authority

Two good verses that illustrate the proper relationship between the Bible and the church very well are Acts 17, vv. 10 and 11. Over the years they have become favorite verses of mine to use in conversations with Roman Catholics because they are so descriptive.

---

6. These health issues could easily be avoided by providing each person a small plastic cup filled with wine.

They read as follows: "Then the brethren immediately sent Paul and Silas away by night to Berea. When they arrived, they went into the synagogue of the Jews. These were more fair-minded than those in Thessalonica, in that they received the word with all readiness, and searched the Scriptures daily to find out *whether these things were so.*"

In these verses we read about how Paul and Barnabas have an encounter with the Jews of Berea. We read that they were more disposed to hearing the message of the apostle than those in Thessalonica, among whom some were moved by envy and got Paul in trouble (Acts 17:5–8). These Jews accepted the message of Paul with all readiness of mind. One could say that these Jews acknowledged Paul's apostolic authority. That is true, but these verses do not stop just there. They say that these Bereans, whom the Bible commends as being noble, even though they accepted Paul's authority, still *double-checked his word against what the Scriptures said.*

This is a very important thing. It means that even though Paul in and of himself has apostolic authority, *it is still a relative authority compared to the ultimate authority of the Scriptures.* Acts 17:10–11 does not put apostolic authority and the Bible's authority onto one plane. It does not acknowledge the Roman Catholic idea that Scripture and tradition are two equal wellsprings of truth. Here we see the Bereans applying the principle of *sola Scriptura* in action: in order to decide a question of faith, they have to match it up with the Scriptures, because ultimately the Scriptures decide all things. Furthermore, these Bereans were using the Old Testament Scriptures, which were there before Paul, before Peter, before the apostolic church, and before the Roman Catholic Church.

## Ex Cathedra?

The council of Vatican I in 1870 claimed that the pope is infallible when speaking on questions of faith and morals. The decree of papal infallibility, as we can see, came very late after the first century of Christianity. That is because this doctrine was never taught, but rather the supremacy of councils was held to when deciding dogmas. That is why the Eastern Orthodox Church, which went on its separate way of theological development after the split of 1054, still holds to the supremacy of councils. Papal infallibility was also opposed by many bishops and theologians, such as Ignaz von Döllinger, who was ultimately silenced by Pope Pius IX, who presided at the council.

## ROMAN CATHOLICISM: MAN SUPPLEMENTS GOD'S WORD

Historically, the Roman Catholic teaching of papal infallibility didn't have much to do with ascertaining God's word. The latter part of the nineteenth century was a time when anti-church ideologies were on the rise, such as liberalism and materialism. For example, Darwin's theory of evolution had been publicized only eleven years previously in 1859. Admittedly, papal infallibility was passed to consolidate papal power to strengthen the church.

When the decree of papal infallibility was read in the Vatican, the sky turned completely black, and it was so dark that the pope had to continue reading the words of the decree with the light of a lantern. Many bishops thought this was a bad omen and went back to their countries in dismay. The decree of papal infallibility caused some fifty thousand Roman Catholics in France and Switzerland to break away from the Roman Catholic Church. They are today known as the Old Catholic Church and can also be found in the United States.

Papal infallibility stems from Rome's faulty epistemology. Some Roman Catholic theologians, such as the rationalist Abelard, claim that certain doctrines are to be believed based on the dictates of reason. This erases the distinction between man and God, and thus creates a chain of being between man and God, something akin to the *demiurge* of the Greek philosophers.[7] Rome teaches that only her priesthood can interpret the Scripture correctly, as though the priesthood has some special, gnostic access to God's thoughts. This also means that the pope also takes a special place along this chain of being. Among all men he is supposed to be the highest up along the chain of being and has a special insight into the knowledge of God.[8] This is the kind of thinking behind papal infallibility.

In effect, the pope can decree new teachings, and what he says is binding on the conscience of men, just as the Scriptures. Nowhere does the Bible affirm such a thing. Infallibility is an exclusive characteristic of God because only God is omniscient. Only God can make infallible statements. Neither the pope nor any other man can share with God in this.

Roman Catholics may respond by saying that the pope is being led by the Holy Spirit when he speaks ex cathedra. But this is beside the point. What the pope decrees infallibly is supposedly known only between himself and God. In other words, it is subjective, just like when charismatics claim that God has spoken to them, privately and personally. As such, it must be

---

7. Sahakian, *History of Philosophy*, 101.
8. Van Til, *Christian Apologetics*, 45–46.

measured by a higher standard, such as the Scriptures. The Spirit comes and goes wherever he wants (John 3:8) and cannot be bound by anyone.

## The Testimony of the Holy Spirit

Rome opposes the doctrine from the Reformation on the illumination of the Holy Spirit in the individual believer. This is important because of the role the Holy Spirit plays in the selection of the canon.

Roman Catholic apologists during the Reformation such as Francis de Sales claimed that the uniform tradition of the Roman Catholic Church was the authoritative basis for the selection of the books that belonged to the biblical canon. Roman Catholic apologists point to differences in interpretation of various Protestant denominations of various doctrines. They claim that the Holy Spirit could not be the author of these differences in interpretation, thus private interpretation is an illegitimate method of interpreting the Bible. These apologists employ a method of skepticism called Pyrrhonism, which says that if one relies on their own intellect, they cannot be sure of anything. This method of skepticism is akin to Descartes's methodological doubt, which says that we can be sure of nothing except our own existence.[9]

De Sales writes about the illumination of the Holy Spirit:

> Good heavens! What obscurity, what dense fog, what shades of night! Are we not now fully enlightened in so important and grave a difference! The question is how one can tell these canonical books; we wish to have some rule to distinguish them, and they offer us something that passes in the interior of the soul, which no one sees, nobody knows save the soul itself and its Creator![10]

De Sales is exasperated by the idea that the Reformers appealed to the truth of the Spirit of the Creator. Obscurity, fog, shades of night. This is mistrust of the Holy Spirit to suggest that the Holy Spirit is not enough to give us the truth; rather, a group of churchmen must do it for us. They offer us something that passes in the interior of the soul, which no one sees, nobody knows, save the soul itself and the church!

The problem with the Roman Catholic argument is that it presupposes that the pope has exclusive direct lines of communication to the

---

9. Woodbridge, *Biblical Authority*, 70–71.
10. De Sales, *Catholic Controversy*, 73–77.

Holy Spirit. It must insert its own ecclesiastical authority between God and man. The Roman Catholic Church also believes that when the pope speaks ex cathedra, he is illuminated by the Holy Spirit as an individual. The Holy Spirit comes and goes where he wishes (John 3:8). Just like the Montanists in earlier centuries, the pope has no authority to tether the Holy Spirit to himself to the exclusion of all other people on earth. If the Holy Spirit can speak to one man, surely, he can speak to another. Since the Holy Spirit is God, he is capable of making men understand his message to them, despite their finitude and frailty.

# Refutation of Roman Catholic Arguments against *Sola Scriptura*

Introduction

OF ALL THE OPPONENTS of *sola Scriptura*, the Roman Catholic Church is the most ardent. It has the most extensive system of argumentation against it. Rome also employs many theologians and writers aiming to oppose and destroy *sola Scriptura*. Therefore, it would be useful to review and counter some of the material that they have published attempting to refute *sola Scriptura*.

One such work is a booklet titled *Scripture Alone? 21 Reasons to Reject Sola Scriptura*, by Joel Peters. In the following, I will analyze this booklet and give a refutation of its arguments against *sola Scriptura*.

Refutation of *21 Reasons to Reject* Sola Scriptura

Some of Peters's arguments have been refuted in previous chapters. The rest I will deal with here. Let us begin by addressing the way Peters defines *sola Scriptura*, since this affects much of his reasoning against it. This is how Peters defines *sola Scriptura*:

> The Bible—*as interpreted by the individual believer*—is the only source of religious authority and *is the Christian's sole rule of faith* or criterion regarding what is to be believed. By this doctrine, which is one of the foundational beliefs of Protestantism, a

## REFUTATION OF ROMAN CATHOLIC ARGUMENTS

Protestant *denies that there is any other source of religious authority or divine Revelation to humanity.*[1]

As to Roman Catholic authority, Peters writes:

> The immediate or direct rule of faith is the teachings of the Church; the Church in turn takes her teaching from divine Revelation—both the written Word, called Sacred Scripture, and the oral or unwritten Word, known as "Tradition." *The teaching authority or "Magisterium" of the Catholic Church (headed by the Pope), although not itself a source of divine Revelation, nevertheless has a God-given mission to interpret and teach both Scripture and Tradition.* Scripture and Tradition are the sources of Christian doctrine, *the Christian's remote or indirect rule of faith.*[2]

This definition is incorrect in the three parts that have been italicized. It is clear that Peters, as many Roman Catholics, does not truly understand *sola Scriptura*. Many of his arguments are attacking a straw man. It appears that he is equating *sola Scriptura* with *solo Scriptura*, which Protestantism rejects. A large segment of Protestantism upholds the authority of church tradition, presbyterian church government authority, science, etc. It is just that we do not put these things on the same level as the Bible. In other words, these are relative authorities with regards to the single highest authority, the Bible.

Since Peters equates *sola Scriptura* with *solo Scriptura*, we can then dispense with nine of the twenty-one chapters he wrote against *sola Scriptura*. Peters repeatedly argues that we must define the Bible first to be able to invoke *sola Scriptura*. But, as described in chapter 4, the material of the Bible is separate from the principle that says that we use only the Bible for hermeneutics as the sole highest authority.

Peters makes the incredible claim that the Roman Catholic Church gave its final, definitive, infallible definition of the biblical canon at the Council of Trent in 1546, naming seven extra books compared to the Protestant canon.[3] This is an incredible statement, which implies that neither Christians nor Jews knew what their Bible was made up of for the great majority of human history. Peters makes a historical error, since by the year 303 believers knew which books belonged to the Bible and which

---

1. Peters, *Scripture Alone*, unnumbered page; emphasis on "rule of faith" in original; all other emphases added.
2. Peters, *Scripture Alone*, unnumbered page.
3. Peters, *Scripture Alone*, 36.

ones didn't. This was the time of the Diocletian persecutions, when the holy books of believing Christians were taken away from them. By this time, Christians knew which books were part of the canon and which ones were secondary.

Furthermore, Peters also claims that there are no internal criteria for determining the canon of the Bible, but that an external authority was necessary to do so—this, besides the other claim that the Bible does not interpret itself, but needs an external interpreter, which is again, the Roman Catholic Church. Peters, as do many other Roman Catholics, wants to bind the correct interpretation of the Bible to their own church. This replaces careful analysis and thought. For Peters, verification of a given doctrine depends upon what kind of lineage a church has, but this can hardly be considered an argument.[4]

In Peters's view, it is as though God is incapable of making himself clear to people, and needs a spokesperson, the pope, to speak for him. It is as if the Holy Spirit did not have the power to do as he pleases and make himself known to individual people. This idea cuts off all lines of communication between God and the individual believer.

In John 8:12–16 we read about how the Pharisees questioned Jesus' authority as he taught in the temple:

> Then Jesus spoke to them again, saying, "I am the light of the world. He who follows Me shall not walk in darkness, but have the light of life." The Pharisees therefore said to Him, "You bear witness of Yourself; Your witness is not true." Jesus answered and said to them, "Even if I bear witness of Myself, My witness is true, for I know where I came from and where I am going; but you do not know where I come from and where I am going. You judge according to the flesh; I judge no one. And yet if I do judge, My judgment is true; for I am not alone, but I am with the Father who sent Me."

Here Jesus says that his and his Father's testimony are enough for him to reveal truth to men. Jesus didn't need any kind of proof to back up what he was saying. This is because he is divine and omniscient. He judges everything but is judged by no man. On the other hand, the church is made up of sinful, fallible men, who all need a guide.

---

4. Many times in the Middle Ages, Roman Catholics argued that their view was represented by the apostle Peter, and that since the other party belonged to a different church or group, they were wrong.

Furthermore, Peters tries to play up the fact that none of the original Bible manuscripts is extant, and that there are thousands of variations in the Bible's text, and that there are hundreds of Bible versions. This may affect the content of the canon, but as described earlier, this ultimately doesn't affect the principle of *sola Scriptura*.

## 2 Timothy 3:16–17

Besides this, Peters argues that *sola Scriptura* is not taught in the Bible, which has been dealt with in this book. However, he references 2 Tim 3:16–17, so let us examine his arguments in more detail.

Peters lists five arguments against 2 Tim 3:16–17 being used in support of *sola Scriptura*. First, he claims that the Greek word ὠφέλιμος (*ophelimos*), which means "profitable," implies that the Scriptures are useful only for doctrine, reproof, correction, instruction in righteousness, to make the man of God perfect. In a similar way, water is useful, even necessary for our survival, but it is not sufficient since we must also eat food. This may sound like a plausible argument. However, neither tradition nor church authority is ever mentioned as having such capabilities. In other words, the word "alone" is not in the text, but the word "Bible" is in the text alone. We never read about tradition making anyone perfect, nor do we read about men of the church making someone perfect, since no man is perfect. This would be reading much too much into the lines between the Bible. Our reason is tainted by sin, but the Bible is not, because it is God's word.

Peters's second and third argument claim that the entire Bible is not represented in 2 Tim 3:16–17. For example, the Greek word πᾶσα (*pasa*) refers to every single book of the Bible, and not the Bible as a whole. Furthermore, Peters makes much of the fact that in Timothy's time only the Old Testament Scriptures were available for believers. Is the Old Testament sufficient for the rule of faith? Can this be said about each book as well?

Let us consider that God did not author the Bible with each book in an isolated context. Each book of the Bible must be read in context with every other book to understand the message of the Bible as a whole. Furthermore, the Old Testament Jews received enough information in the Old Testament that they could know who Jesus Christ was. The Old Testament prophets spoke about him and about the events surrounding his birth, life, death, and resurrection.

For example, the proto-gospel in Gen 3 describes how God slew an animal to make clothes for Adam and Eve. The skin of a dead animal foreshadowed the animal sacrifices of the priestly system in Leviticus. Just as the skin of a slain animal covered Adam and Eve's shame and nudity, so does Christ's external righteousness cover our iniquities. We could mention Luke 24:25–32 wherein we read about how Jesus revealed himself to the two travelers to Emmaus. In v. 27 we read, "And beginning at Moses and all the prophets, he expounded unto them in all the scriptures the things concerning himself."

Jude 3 says, "Beloved, while I was very diligent to write to you concerning our common salvation, I found it necessary to write to you exhorting you to contend earnestly for *the faith which was once for all delivered to the saints*." This means that by the time that Jude wrote his letter to his readers, the Christian faith had already been delivered unto believers. This is a kind of faith that Christian believers can stand upon and be complete in, fully equipped for all good works. Yet the Letter of Jude goes on. This illustrates that even a portion of the Scripture less than the whole can make the Christian complete. Nothing like this is said of oral tradition. Indeed, the Holy Scriptures, though written by men, are the word of God. The traditions of men are just that—men's words, and only men's words, not God's words.[5]

Peters's fourth argument is related to the first in that the Bible alone is not mentioned as being perfect. We have dealt with this already. Perhaps we could also mention that according to Peters, Jas 1:4 states that patience makes a man perfect. But then this means that the Roman Catholic Church's three-legged stool is now a four-legged stool!

Peters makes the unusual claim that 2 Tim 3:16–17 is only about the man of God being a clergyman, implying that it is only the clergy's job to interpret the Bible. However, the term "man of God" is a broad term. Just as the Jewish people are God's (Old Testament) people, any believer in Christ may be considered a man of God.

## The Canon

Since Peters claims that Protestants left out seven books from the canon, whereas the Roman Catholic Church has seventy-three, we will deal with this briefly.

5. Mueller, *Called to Believe*, 37.

The following is a list of internal characteristics that help define a particular book as part of the Bible:

- The book itself claims to be the word of God.
- The book is free of theological, historical, logical, and any other kinds of errors.
- The book is consistent with other books of the Bible.
- The book endeavors to increase holiness and knowledge of God.

Cardinal Cajetan in Luther's time had this to say about the seven apocryphal books (Tobias, Judith, Baruch, Wisdom, Ecclesiasticus, and 1 and 2 Maccabees):

> Here we close our commentaries on the historical books of the Old Testament. For the rest (that is, Judith, Tobit, and the books of Maccabees) are counted by St Jerome out of the canonical books, and are placed amongst the Apocrypha, along with Wisdom and Ecclesiasticus, as is plain from the *Prologus Galeatus*. Nor be thou disturbed, like a raw scholar, if thou shouldest find anywhere, either in the sacred councils or the sacred doctors, these books reckoned as canonical. For the words as well of councils as of doctors are to be reduced to the correction of Jerome. Now, according to his judgment, in the epistle to the bishops Chromatius and Heliodorus, these books (and any other like books in the canon of the Bible) are not canonical, that is, not in the nature of a rule for confirming matters of faith.[6]

Besides Cajetan, such early theologians as Origen, Tertullian, Athanasius, and Jerome rejected what is known as the Apocrypha (from the Greek ἀπόκρυφος, *apókruphos*, meaning hidden, unrecognized, or uncanonical, from even before the Reformation). In later centuries, Cardinal Zomenes and Pope Gregory the Great also rejected these books as canonical. About the Apocrypha, Cajetan remarked that they were stories that could be used for edification but were nothing that doctrine could be built upon.[7]

Furthermore, the books of Wisdom and Ecclesiasticus contain Protestant doctrines. For example, Wis 15:7 reads: "The potter also, tempering soft earth, with labour fashioneth every vessel for our service, and of the same clay he maketh both vessels that are for clean uses, and likewise

---

6. Cardinal Cajetan, "Commentary on all the Authentic Historical Books of the Old Testament," cited by Whitaker, *Disputation on Holy Scripture*, 424.

7. Cserhati, *Refuting Rome*, 47–48.

such as serve to the contrary: but what is the use of these vessels, the potter is the judge." Tobias contradicts the message of salvation in the true Bible; 1 and 2 Maccabees and the additions to Esther also have contradictions. Jerome mentions that the book of Baruch was a later addition to the book of Jeremiah.

Peters makes the argument that the New Testament either alludes to or directly quotes the seven books of the Apocrypha not less than 150 times. This may sound like a convincing argument, but the Bible also mentions other books besides the seven apocryphal books. For example, Josh 10:13 and 2 Sam 1:18 both mention the book of Jasher:

> So the sun stood still, and the moon stopped, till the people had revenge Upon their enemies. *Is this not written in the Book of Jasher? So the sun stood still in the midst of heaven, and did not hasten to go down for about a whole day.* (Josh 10:13)

If the Holy Spirit had truly guided the Roman Catholic Church in correctly assembling the canon, they should have also included the book of Jasher. They didn't, so therefore the Roman Catholic canon was not led by the Holy Spirit.

### *Sola Scriptura* and Luther's Emotional Problems?

Peters makes the surprising claim that the doctrine of *sola Scriptura* was born because Luther wanted to be freed from feelings of guilt and despair. He claims that to be free of his conscience, Luther then formulated the doctrine of *sola fide*, meaning that we are saved by faith alone, apart from doing good works and avoiding sin as a necessary component of our salvation, as taught by the Roman Catholic Church. So therefore, since the Roman Catholic Church asserted what Luther was incapable of doing, in desperation he rejected the authority of the church.

Now, it is only a natural desire of man to wish to be free of guilt, temptation, and despair. Luther might have taken things too far in being overly scrupulous in examining his conscience, as is the case with some Roman Catholic confession-goers. Luther was trying to be consistent with God's command in the Bible to be holy as he is holy (1 Pet 1:16). Of course, he fell into despair—who wouldn't?

It was when Luther read Rom 1:17 that he realized that the just shall live by faith, also echoed in the Old Testament, in Hab 2:4. It was when

## REFUTATION OF ROMAN CATHOLIC ARGUMENTS

he realized that this is the true message of salvation in the Bible that he attained inner peace.[8] In his own words, Luther states, "I felt myself to be reborn and to have gone through open doors into paradise."[9]

In summary, Luther underwent psychological torments precisely because Rome's way of salvation that he was trying to implement as a monk kept him from having any peace. When he finally understood the true message of salvation as described in the Bible, this gave him peace.

Luther isn't the only one who formulated the principle of *sola Scriptura*, as even Peters himself states that Wycliffe, who preceded Luther by a century and a half, also believed this doctrine, along with many others before him. As we have also shown in a previous chapter, Luther was only one of many theologians in the church who advocated for the supreme authority of the Scriptures in the life of the church.[10]

### Heretical Movements Based Their Doctrines on Scripture Alone

Peters makes the claim that *sola Scriptura* must be wrong, since some heretical movements in the Middle Ages based their doctrines on Scripture alone, apart from tradition and the teaching authority of the church. For example, he cites how Victor, bishop of Rome, threatened to excommunicate a large part of the Eastern Church since they disagreed with the date when Easter should be celebrated. However, his decree went largely unheeded in the church.

Besides not being able to substantiate tradition as a separate source of truth apart from Scripture, this argument is very much lacking. Peters makes the argument that we cannot be sure that the interpretation of any part of Scripture of any Protestant is true. In a way, we can be comforted by this, because this would lead us into the error of *sola ecclesia*, the self-same error that Rome is in. We could ask the self-same question about Roman Catholic doctrine and Roman authority, as to how they know for sure that their interpretation of any part of the Bible (i.e., Matt 16:16–18) is correct, or how they know that the Holy Spirit is with them.

The fact is that many so-called heretical movements in the Middle Ages, whether they were truly heretical, such as the Bogomils or the Cathars, or possibly evangelical, such as the Waldenses, or Henry the monk

8. Kittelson, *Luther the Reformer*, 91–99.
9. Bainton, *Here I Stand*, 49–51.
10. Mathison, *Shape of Sola Scriptura*, 102.

reacted against the pomp, wealth, and luxury of the Roman Catholic Church hierarchy, and against sexual immorality.

For example, some priests held concubines and were unable to keep their vows when celibacy was imposed in the late eleventh century. These people reacted to the excess of the Roman Catholic Church in those days by attempting to return to apostolic poverty and pure living. This is why, for example, Valdes of Lyons gave away his possessions to the poor, to imitate the apostles of the early church, from which many in the Roman Catholic Church had departed.

In fact, some of these heretical groups departed from *sola Scriptura*. For example, Fra Dolcino, a prominent member of the Apostolic Brethren, based his teachings not only on the Bible but also on the works of other Middle Age mystics, and believed that he received direct divine revelation from God.[11] Marguerite Porete, another Middle Age heretic burned for her heresy, believed that she could communicate directly with God, and described the soul's mystical ascent to God in seven stages in her book, *Mirror of Simple Souls*.[12]

Some of these religious groups preached anti-clerical sermons against the Roman Catholic priests, which provoked the church to persecute these mendicant groups. Pope John XXII even declared apostolic poverty heretical in 1323.[13] To accuse these dissident Middle Age religious groups of heresy, just because they exposed and chastised the sins of the Roman Catholic clergy, is simply wrong.

Some of these groups, such as the Bogomils or the Cathars, were truly heretical, because they held to horrendous doctrines, such as the teachings that God and the devil are dualist deities, and that the devil created the world, as well as the rejection of marriage, baptism, and the Old Testament.[14] The fact that any of these groups may have held to what may seem to be something somewhat like *Sola Scriptura* is purely incidental to their set of beliefs. *Sola Scriptura* did not make these groups heretical, but rather the anti-biblical content of their beliefs did.

---

11. Frassetto, *Great Medieval Heretics*, 122.
12. Frassetto, *Great Medieval Heretics*, 142–44.
13. Frassetto, *Great Medieval Heretics*, 125.
14. Frassetto, *Great Medieval Heretics*, 13–20.

# Comparison of Major Ideological Currents That Deny *Sola Scriptura*

SOMEONE ONCE CHARACTERIZED THE Roman Catholic Church, liberal theology, and the charismatic movement as a triple chord that cannot be broken. Despite their apparent differences, these three ideological currents share much in common, and are diverse manifestations of the fundamental denial of *sola Scriptura*. The table below sums up their main traits that put them on equal footing with one another, but in direct contradiction with *sola Scriptura*.

Table 6. Comparison of major trends that deny *sola Scriptura*

| Roman Catholicism | Charismatic Movement | Theological Liberalism |
|---|---|---|
| | Denial of *Sola Scriptura* | |
| Humanism: Bible subject to church | Humanism: Bible subject to experience | Humanism: Bible subject to human understanding |
| Tradition added to Scripture | Extra-biblical revelations | Modern science is an authority besides Scripture |
| Ritualism | Ritualism: Prayer in Jesus' name only, altar call, sinner's prayer | Dead rituals |
| Papism: Holy Spirit tied to pope (supramontanism) | Montanism: Holy Spirit tied to the believer | Reason above the Holy Spirit |
| Ecumenism | Ecumenism | Ecumenism |
| Holy Spirit bound to the priesthood | The Bible becomes alive only through the Holy Spirit | Barthianism: The Bible becomes the living word through faith |

Roman Catholicism is characterized by her high church rituals. The charismatic movement is characterized by its lack of formalism and its experientialism. Romanism delves into mysticism. Both are characteristically gnostic in bypassing the Scriptures to reach God. Liberalism is characterized by its cold academic dissection and evisceration of the Bible.

Not by adding to the Bible per se does liberalism contradict *sola Scriptura*, rather by elevating the academic opinions of scientists and theologians next to the Bible. Similar to the Roman Catholic Church, only specially trained theologians are able to correctly interpret the Bible for the laity. Charismatic believers think that only they are "in the know" with their special, direct (gnostic) access to divine knowledge.

These three movements communicate with one another. They attend conferences with one another. Charismatic leaders pray together with Pope Francis, and approximately 10 percent of Roman Catholics are charismatic. This number is constantly rising. There are many women liberal pastors in certain charismatic denominations.

Despite accusations of spiritual deadness, charismatics borrow this idea from the liberals, despite the Bible's clear teaching that a pastor "must be blameless, the husband of one wife" (1 Tim 3:2). The charismatic movement appeals to a vibrant emotionalism, but does it suspect that liberals do as well? Only to a different Jesus, not found in the pages of Scripture. Charismatics claim that they receive a word from God, yet the Roman Catholic Church outdoes them all in the very person of the pope, who claims that he is infallible when speaking on faith and morals.

The charismatic movement claims that the Holy Spirit cannot be hindered by dogma, rituals, rules, formalism, or denominational boundaries. Thus, ecumenism becomes the great byword in charismatic circles.

However, charismatics still have demands for a local monopoly on the Holy Spirit, as opposed to "half-Christian" denominations. Rome "allows" other denominations to call themselves churches with a false graciousness, but still calls them sects and separated brethren, claiming herself to be the only true church with the fullness of revelation and authority.

Liberals, on the other hand, stand the most to lose. First jettisoning biblical inerrancy, nothing is left of the Christian religion for them but an empty shell. Liberals attempt to compromise to be well liked by the world, but by doing so concede defeat and become God's enemies (Jas 4:4). They also become repugnant in the world's eyes. Well-known atheist Sam Harris correctly points out their error in that if someone is consistently liberal, they must ultimately reject the faith.[1] Since liberal theology plays by their opponent's rules, they must necessarily lose. To take Scripture less and less seriously means to eventually become an atheist.

All three movements deprecate the Bible, and by doing so they lose their vitality. Roman Catholicism ends up in repetitious, vain rituals and lengthy prayers. The charismatic movement also ends up in ritualistic altar calls, repetitious praying in tongues. Liberal theology merely goes through the motions since it is devoid of meaning and truth content.

These are several ways that these three movements/churches feed into one another's spirituality, in a direction away from Scripture. This is the sad reality when one rejects the teaching of *sola Scriptura*.

---

1. Harris, *Letter to Christian Nation*, 103–6.

# Eastern Orthodoxy: A Mix of Mysticism

> And do not be conformed to this world, but be transformed by the renewing of your mind, that you may prove what is that good and acceptable and perfect will of God.
>
> ROM 12:2

## Introduction

THE EASTERN ORTHODOX CHURCH has approximately 185 million adherents worldwide, located mainly in Russia and Eastern Europe, although 25 million Orthodox believers are found in the Western world, 5 million of these in the United States. This church will be dealt with in this book because of its sizable number of followers as well as its denial of the principle of *sola Scriptura* and because Eastern Orthodox apologists polemicize against it, and because some Protestants are converting to Eastern Orthodoxy.

The history of the Eastern Orthodox Church is tied to the development of the church in the Eastern half of the Roman Empire. The Eastern Orthodox Church holds early theologians in great esteem, such as Basil of Caesarea and Gregory of Nazianzus. Due to ever-widening political, cultural, and theological differences with the West, this church split with the Roman Catholic Church in 1054 when Cardinal Humbert of Silva Candida and Ecumenical Patriarch of Constantinople Michael Cerularius mutually excommunicated one another.[1] Afterwards, the Eastern and Western Churches developed independently from one another, and have thus accrued several differences in their doctrines, besides some similarities.

---

1. González, *Early Church*, 313.

# EASTERN ORTHODOXY: A MIX OF MYSTICISM

## Overview of the Eastern Orthodox Religion

Eastern Orthodoxy is classified as apophatic theology. *Apophatic theology* describes God in negative terms. In other words, apophatic theology says what God is not. This is because Eastern Orthodoxy believes that God is so transcendent, so incomprehensible, that the divine essence is basically unknowable. Eastern Orthodox treats the reasoning mind with suspicion, and therefore tends towards the exact opposite pole, that of mysticism. Since God cannot be known, one can know God only in a mysterious encounter. Referring to Gregory of Nyssa, Eastern Orthodoxy holds that "God's name is not known; it is wondered at." We cannot figure out God logically; rather, he is revealed through a mystery for our understanding.

Unfortunately, this way mysticism leads people away from studying, meditating upon, and understanding the Scriptures.[2] Quite similarly to the charismatic movement, human experience takes precedence over the testimony of Scripture. If God is completely unknowable, this means that we could even do away with the Bible entirely.

## The Eastern Orthodox View of Authority

Let us examine the teaching of the Eastern Orthodox Church on authority. This is important, because the Eastern Orthodox Church uses similar arguments to attempt to refute *sola Scriptura*. The Eastern Orthodox teach that various things contribute to authoritative teaching, including:

- The Bible
- The first seven ecumenical councils
- Later councils with their dogmatic statements
- The writings of the early theologians
- Canon law
- Church liturgy, including service books, icons, church government, worship, and art[3]

The reason the Orthodox Church holds to the authority of all these things is because it looks upon itself as the heir to the great heritage of

---

2. K. Ware, *Orthodox Way*, 14–15.

3. Letham, *Through Western Eyes*, 174; Clendenin, *Eastern Orthodox Christianity*, 108.

the ancient (catholic) church, which was active for the first few centuries in the Eastern Roman Empire. For example, the first seven ecumenical councils were held in cities in the east: Nicea, Constantinople, Ephesus, and Chalcedon.

As opposed to the Roman Catholic Church, the Eastern Orthodox Church has no single head, no pope. Instead, so-called patriarchs are major ecclesiastical leaders, bishops in larger cities, such as Moscow. This patriarchate is a remnant of the patriarchates of the early Christian church, with five centers located in Alexandria, Jerusalem, Antioch, Constantinople, and Rome. Each patriarchate is autocephalous in nature, meaning that it alone has the right to determine what happens within its own jurisdiction. As opposed to the papacy, no one patriarch can take control over the rest of the church. In fact, this is why the Orthodox claim that even the Roman Catholic pope as the patriarch of Rome was part of the Orthodox Church but broke away from it because he demanded supreme power over all the church. Church dogma must be decided by all the patriarchs acting in concert with one another.

Similar to the Roman Catholic Church, the Orthodox Church also treats Scripture merely as a part of tradition. As we have seen, the Eastern Orthodox Church puts a list of other things besides the Scripture, in the belief that the Bible and church doctrine do not contradict one another.

This is a denial of *sola Scriptura*, because it is a case of concordance (which was dealt with earlier), which teaches that there are several sources of binding authority besides the Scriptures. Hence the Scriptures are no longer the *sole* highest authority. Orthodox writers may affirm, however, that Scripture holds the primary position among all other forms of tradition, going so far as to say that it is "the supreme expression of God's revelation," and that Scripture has first place, and that Scripture and tradition are unequal in value. But they are only being inconsistent when they also say that the interpretation of Scripture is "the mind of the church," or that it is explained and applied in holy tradition.[4]

Just like Rome, they claim that Scripture and tradition have equal authority and are equally valid, quoting John Chrysostom: "[The apostles] did not deliver all things by epistle, but many things also unwritten, and in like manner both the one and the other worthy of credit."[5] Also, just

---

4. K. Ware, *Orthodox Way*, 110.

5. Clendenin, *Eastern Orthodox Christianity*, 112. Note that Chrysostom lived in the fourth century, when views on the relationship between Scripture and tradition had

like Rome, the Eastern Orthodox Church rejects the private interpretation of Scripture, saying that the human mind is not like a "tabula rasa" but that the Bible is interpreted according to their tradition, councils, and church leaders.[6]

The Eastern Orthodox Church views Rome as subjecting tradition to the pope. They also criticize the Protestant churches for placing Scripture above tradition. For the Eastern Church, it is the Holy Spirit working in the church that is the authority. For the Eastern Orthodox Church, authority is not dogmatic, but rather pneumatic, or even charismatic.[7]

In the Eastern Orthodox Church, the incarnation of Jesus Christ and the operation of the Holy Spirit bring the fullness of revelation. All the above-mentioned sources of authority are a faculty attributed to the Holy Spirit, who reveals these things to men.[8] The Holy Spirit is believed to reveal truth not just in the form of words, but also in images such as icons. Hence the large emphasis on iconic imagery in the Eastern Orthodox Church, which is also a focal point in their worship and liturgy.

Dogma cannot be understood separately from human experience in Eastern Orthodoxy. As such, according to Eastern Orthodoxy, certain parts of the Bible are more useful than others. For example, Isaiah is more useful than Ecclesiastes, and John is more useful than Jude.[9] But this is a form of differentiation within the Scripture, where one verse has a higher value than another. God's word does not trump God's word, because every single verse of the Bible has the same weight, and the entire testimony of Scripture must be considered. One cannot just pick and choose his favorite verse.

Similar to Rome, Eastern Orthodoxy also rejects the sole highest authority of Scripture, that is, *sola Scriptura*. This is due to the multiple sources of authority that it holds to. Eastern Orthodoxy uses polemics against *sola Scriptura* similar to those of the Roman Catholic Church. These include arguments that the Scriptures themselves don't teach that they are "all sufficient," and that they rely on various extra-biblical

---

already changed since the first century. Naturally, nobody can cite these unwritten words of tradition.

6. K. Ware, *Orthodox Way*, 110.

7. The Eastern Orthodox view of the Protestant view is incorrect, since, for example, according to question 4 of the Larger Catechism of the Westminster Standards, "the Spirit of God bearing witness by and with the Scriptures in the heart of man, is alone able fully to persuade it that they are the very Word of God" (M. Smith, *Harmony*, 13).

8. Letham, *Through Western Eyes*, 178.

9. Letham, *Through Western Eyes*, 186.

traditions, or that Scripture was the basis of the early church, or that Christians can interpret the Bible for themselves without the aid of the church. Eastern Orthodoxy also repeats the devious claim that Protestantism cannot be right because there are so many different Protestant denominations.[10] These arguments were dealt with in previous chapters, so these arguments will not be dealt with again here.

It might be worth noting that though both the Eastern Orthodox and Roman Catholic Churches claim apostolic succession ever since the early days of the church, so does the Anglican Church, which is a Protestant ecclesiastical body. Anglican bishops trace their own lineage by the laying on of hands, and name by name all the way back to the apostles.

## Criticism of the Eastern Orthodox View of Authority

The Orthodox Church has an incorrect view of scriptural authority because it is not based on *sola Scriptura*. First, just as with the Roman Catholic view, it includes Scripture as a part of an all-encompassing tradition. We must reiterate that the Scriptures predate and make the church and not the other way around. Second Peter 3:15–16 says the following:

> As also our beloved brother Paul, according to the wisdom given to him, has written to you, as also in all his epistles, speaking in them of these things, in which are some things hard to understand, which untaught and unstable people twist to their own destruction, as they do also *the rest of the Scriptures*.

This verse demonstrates that already in the very time of the apostles the content of the Scriptures was known. No pope nor council was necessary later to determine this.

While it may be true that the information contained in the Scriptures came from the writers themselves, still, the same information emanated originally as a corpus from the mind of God before all time. It is this pure information from God that alone is completely reliable as opposed to the word of any priest, pope, pastor, or patriarch. We can refer to Acts 17:10–11, which says that the believers verified even Paul's words based on the Scriptures, which are a higher authority than even the apostles.

Human experience is not on the same level as God's word. This would make something within the human frame as divine as God's word. If we

---

10. Whiteford, *Sola Scriptura*.

judge God's word based on our own experience, that violates basic biblical exegesis. We could make the Bible say anything we want it to say.

It is also incorrect to say that some parts of the Bible are more useful than others. This leads directly to picking and choosing parts of the Bible that we prefer over others. Let us remember the words of 2 Tim 3:16: "All Scripture is given by inspiration of God, and is profitable for doctrine, for reproof, for correction, for instruction in righteousness." If we pit one portion of Scripture against another, then this means that there would be a hierarchy of verses of increasing importance. This would mean that there would be at least one verse in the Bible which is the least important of all. As such, it could be superseded by all other verses of greater importance. Thus, it could be ignored. This would be like how later versions of the Qur'an revised earlier ones.[11] But the God of the Bible does not lie or contradict or forget himself.

This breaks the principle of *tota Scriptura*. The Eastern Orthodox position creates hierarchical structuring within the Bible itself, with some portions having more authority than others. Different parts are on different levels of authority than the rest. All verses in the Bible have equal importance because it is the same God who inspired all the verses of the entire Bible. Therefore, when formulating any kind of doctrine, all verses must be taken together. Whereas it may be true that some Bible verses are clearer than others, and must be interpreted in light of them, this still does not detract from their equal authority. For a verse to be less important than another is different than to be less clear. Once elucidated by other verses, a hard-to-understand verse does not gain any authority over another one.

---

11. White, *What Every Christian Needs*, 254–63.

# Dispensationalism: Cutting the Scriptures in Half

> You are sons of the prophets, and of the covenant which God made with our fathers, saying to Abraham, "And in your seed all the families of the earth shall be blessed."
>
> ACTS 3:25

## Introduction

A BRAND OF THEOLOGY that is very widespread, especially in the United States, is called dispensationalism, in opposition to covenantal theology. It comes in many varieties, which can all be characterized by three basic tenets:

1. Human history can be divided into multiple dispensations, each with its own economy of salvation. These dispensations are usually listed as: innocence, conscience, human government, promise, law, grace (the church age), and the kingdom (the millennium).

2. God has two people: the Jewish people, who will inherit the earth, and the church, who will inherit the heavens.

3. God has divided his word into two separate parts, one for the Jews and another for the church. To read the Bible properly, one must be able to properly divide the word of truth.[1]

---

1. Ryrie, *Dispensationalism*, 46–47.

## DISPENSATIONALISM: CUTTING THE SCRIPTURES IN HALF

Dispensationalism is tied to the Plymouth Brethren Bible teacher John Nelson Darby (1800–1882). Darby's views are a late innovation in the church, not taught by the early church.[2] This is a strong indication that dispensationalism is incorrect.

Many so-called fundamentalist churches are followers of dispensational theology. The name "fundamentalist" is somewhat hard to define, and has been abused, pejoratively, through ignorance more than it has been used properly. It is interesting to note that in many debates the term "fundamentalist" never gets defined.

In a sense, anyone can be a "fundamentalist." Even liberal atheists. This is because every man has an irreducible, subjectively defined set of axioms that form his belief system. For atheists, this is the belief that "nature is everything," founded on the ever-shifting sands of human reason. The Roman Catholic Church can also be labelled as a fundamentalist church, since they hold that the church was established on a man, Peter, alleged to be the first pope. All Christians are fundamentalists, since they believe the principle of *sola Scriptura*, namely, that the Scriptures are the sole highest authority.

However, when we talk about the fundamentalist movement, we are speaking about a movement, including mainly Presbyterian and Baptist churches starting from the early twentieth century, in opposition to modernist movements, such as evolution and liberal theology, and which hold to the so-called Five Fundamentals, as established by the Presbyterian General Assembly in 1910 in response to the liberalism of Union Theological Seminary.[3] These five fundamentals are:

1. Biblical inspiration and the infallibility of the Bible
2. The virgin birth of Christ
3. Christ's atoning death for sin
4. The bodily resurrection of Jesus Christ
5. The historical miracles of Jesus Christ

However, many nonfundamentalist denominations also hold to these beliefs. What is also largely characteristic of the fundamentalist movement is, besides their dispensationalism, their adherence to a strict literal interpretation of the Bible—strict in the sense that a verse must be taken literally,

---

2. Gerstner, *Wrongly Dividing the Word*, 1–5.
3. Marsden, *Fundamentalism and American Culture*, 117.

unless it is obviously symbolic.[4] Some accuse other denominations of liberal tendencies just because they don't interpret the Bible in this manner.

This is incorrect, because the Bible is, physically speaking, a long sequence of Hebrew and Greek letters. These letters form sentences, chapters, and books. Some sense must be made of the words, so therefore any method of interpretation can be used to make sense of the Bible. However, not all methods make sense, and some make more sense than others. Hence that view is the most conservative (biblical) that makes the most sense of the biblical text.

We must also be cautious not to slide over to the other side of the saddle (a Hungarian figure of speech). We cannot equate conservativism with the Bible itself. If we go too far, we may end up in hyper-orthodoxy, which itself is an error.

The entire Bible cannot be taken strictly literally. The book of Revelation is full of obvious symbols, such as the four living creatures full of eyes (Rev 4:6). Jesus uses parables often to convey his message. For example, he identifies himself as the "door of the sheep" (John 10:7). Whereas Genesis is a history book, the book of Revelation is topical, since it contains many recurring themes, or topics. These themes do not follow a literal timeline, just like events in a dream (or a vision, as is the book of Revelation) do not follow a literal timeline.[5]

Dispensationalism also goes hand in hand with premillennial eschatology, as the millennium is the final dispensation. Furthermore, dispensationalists are also overwhelmingly Arminian in their soteriology.

Since fundamentalist dispensationalists consider themselves staunch conservative theologians, they would wholeheartedly claim that they are strict adherents to the principle of *sola Scriptura*.

Sadly, this is not the case.

## What Is Fundamentally Wrong with Dispensationalism?

Unfortunately, dispensationalism errs in its most elementary tenets. Since it *divides* the Scriptures between the Jews and the church, this means that the entire Bible is no longer the sole highest authority for all people, only parts of it: some parts for some people, other parts for other people. It is important to understand here that when a dispensational theologian "divides"

---

4. Gerstner, *Wrongly Dividing the Word*, 69.
5. Beale with Campbell, *Revelation*, 10–17.

God's word, he is imposing an authority "higher than Scripture" onto the Scriptures themselves. His division of the Bible serves as a lens through which he interprets the Bible. Of course, there is no higher authority than the whole Bible. Therefore, individual dispensational theologians are imposing their own human authority on the Bible, acting as a judge above Scripture. Dispensationalism breaks the teaching of *tota Scriptura, and thus Sola Scriptura as well*. It is no wonder that many different dispensationalist theologies exist, each of which divides human history into different sets of dispensations. Again, error breeds a multitude of views.

The way dispensationalism contradicts *sola Scriptura* is not apparent at first glance, because most people are accustomed to detecting a denial of this doctrine by adding things to the Bible. Dispensationalism is a bit peculiar in that it *detracts* from the unity of the Scriptures due to its inherent character.

The dividing of God's word into different segments has the effect in some churches that they ignore the entire counsel of God. This kind of thought is behind the so-called "New Testament churches," which ignore the Old Testament and accept only the New Testament as authoritative in forming doctrine.

Dispensationalism divides, separates, and isolates. Covenant theology connects and unifies. It presents a holistic, integrated, consistent, big picture of redemptive history. Not so dispensationalism. Dispensationalism is a theologically fragmented system, and not the true theology of the Bible.

## One People, One Covenant

What does the Bible say instead? God does not establish isolated dispensations with the Jews or the gentiles. Instead, he establishes a single covenant with men, which is continuously being developed to an ever-higher level of realization at each step.[6] God first established a covenant with mankind in general through Adam. This is the covenant of works. Adam was told that he could eat from any tree in the garden, except for the tree of the knowledge of good and evil. As long as he did so, he would live. But since he rebelled, he was punished with death.[7]

With the covenant of Noah, God promised he would never destroy the world again. This was the covenant of the preservation of the human

6. Robertson, *Christ of the Covenants*, 29.
7. Riddlebarger, *Case for Amillennialism*, 61.

race and is eternal in character: "The rainbow shall be in the cloud, and I will look on it to remember *the everlasting covenant* between God and every living creature of all flesh that is on the earth" (Gen 9:16). God established this covenant not with one man but with one family.

God establishes the everlasting covenant of grace between himself and Abraham's descendants, representing now a people: "And I will establish My covenant between Me and you and your descendants after you in their generations, for an *everlasting covenant*, to be God to you and your descendants after you" (Gen 17:7).

This everlasting covenant continues into the New Testament: "Now may the God of peace who brought up our Lord Jesus from the dead, that great Shepherd of the sheep, through the blood of the *everlasting covenant*" (Heb 13:20). God does not make mistakes, and he is capable of carrying out his plan. "Jesus Christ is the same yesterday, today and forever" (Heb 13:8). There is only one covenant.

God has only one people, not two. Jews and gentiles are both God's people, inseparable from one another. Christ cannot be rent asunder. This is reflected in 1 Cor 12:27-28: "Now you are the body of Christ, and members individually. And God has appointed these in the church: first *apostles*, second *prophets*, third teachers, after that miracles, then gifts of healings, helps, administrations, varieties of tongues."

Jesus Christ does not have two separate bodies—that would be nonsensical. In this body we have the prophets of the Old Testament as well as the apostles representing the church in the New Testament. These two offices make up the one, single, indivisible body of Christ.

Acts 3:25 demonstrates this even further: "You are *sons of the prophets, and of the covenant which God made with our fathers*, saying to Abraham, 'And in your seed all the families of the earth shall be blessed.'" This means that Luke's audience, the gentile church, are all members of the everlasting covenant described previously, made between God and Adam, Noah, and Abraham.

Acts 7:38 has this to say about the covenant: "This is he who was in *the congregation in the wilderness* with the Angel who spoke to him on Mount Sinai, and with our fathers, the one who received the living oracles to give to us." In Greek, the word for congregation is ἐκκλησία (*ekklesia*), which is commonly used to refer to the church. This church wandering the wilderness is the Jewish nation in the book of Numbers, wandering from Mount Sinai on their way to the promised land.

## DISPENSATIONALISM: CUTTING THE SCRIPTURES IN HALF

Besides establishing a single covenant with his one people, there is only one Mediator (Acts 4:12), one salvation (John 14:6), one Christ. There is only one, and no other. God doesn't have two programs of salvation. Everything is unified in God's plan. If God indeed had two people, it would be sinful of them to be separate from one another, just as Peter sinned by associating with the Jews at Antioch yet keeping aloof from the gentiles (Gal 2:11–14).

So-called "replacement theology" has nothing to do with anti-Semitism. Some Jews who convert to Christianity come to believe in covenant theology, meaning that it truly doesn't have anything to do with anti-Semitism. It is an inaccurate term. Since covenant theology holds to a universal church age, this simply means that the Jews are *the church of the Old Testament* (Acts 7:38). The New Testament church includes believers who are both ethnically Jewish, who trust in the Messiah, and the gentile believers (John 10:16). The Jews have a special advantage in that to them were committed the oracles of God, the prophets, and the law (Rom 3:1–2). There is no partiality with God (Rom 2:11). God loves all nations, equally.

### A Hedge around the Law

In an endeavor to keep from breaking God's law, many fundamentalists put a secondary hedge around God's law. For example, some of them restrict their members from even going to the theater or from drinking alcohol, even though the Bible doesn't forbid either thing. They do this so as not to give the flesh any chance to sin. They reason that if they keep the secondary law, then they'll be safe from breaking the primary law.

This is like how a house is surrounded by a fence, as seen in fig. 7. The house represents the dwelling place of the Christian in the house of God. The fence represents the law. The law is good because it keeps evil from getting in. However, if the Christian climbs over the fence, by breaking the law, then he is subjecting himself to all the dangers outside the house of the Lord. God put the law around the house to show what man can and cannot do.

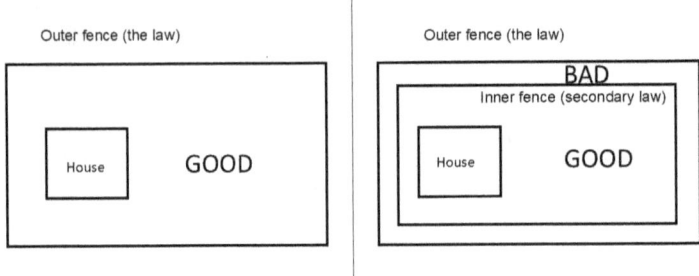

Figure 7. Why is it bad to introduce a secondary law? You end up calling evil what is good (Isa 5:20).

This is a faulty view of both God's word and human nature. To be human is to be a sinner. Even though someone may be saved by grace, that person still harbors remnants of sin within their nature, albeit less and less. But it means that even believers still sin. As such, it doesn't matter whether there is a secondary or tertiary hedge or whatnot to keep us from sinning.

Furthermore, setting up a secondary hedge around the law contradicts God's word. In effect it is saying that what God has called good is bad. This way those fundamentalists who raise this secondary hedge are placing their own man-made laws above God's law. This is wrong. It also shuts them off from God's blessings by avoiding those good areas of God's word that they have designated as bad.

Remember what the serpent said to Eve when he was tempting her to sin: "Has God indeed said, 'You shall not eat of every tree of the garden'?" (Gen 3:1). Observe Eve's response: "We may eat the fruit of the trees of the garden; but of the fruit of the tree which is in the midst of the garden, God has said, 'You shall not eat it, *nor shall you touch it*, lest you die'" (Gen 3:2–3).

Eve added to God's law by saying that God had forbidden her and Adam *to even touch the fruit*. This is false, according to Gen 2:16–17: "And the Lord God commanded the man, saying, 'Of every tree of the garden you may freely eat; but of the tree of the knowledge of good and evil you shall not eat, for in the day that you eat of it you shall surely die.'"

While the intent of these fundamentalists to avoid sin is praiseworthy, they do it incorrectly by negating God's word. "What God has cleansed you must not call common" (Acts 10:15).

To keep God's law a Christian person should be mature enough to practice self-control (Gal 5:13; 2 Pet 1:6). They should know their limits.

For example, if someone can control themselves enough so as not to go past a single glass of alcohol at a party, then by no means are they sinning by having that glass of alcohol.

## Why Is the Rapture Anti-Gospel?

To fully understand the consequences of dispensational thinking, let us examine how this thinking distorts the gospel message. Dispensationalists divide history, the Bible, and the people of God. In the dispensationalist timeline, a relatively short "church age" is interjected into a larger Jewish dispensation (see fig. 8). Dispensationalists typically state that the church age is bookended by two so-called "parentheses." It's as if the church, representing the saving message of the gospel, is a sideshow only, not the main message.

If there is any verse in the Bible that describes a kind of rapture-like event, it can be found in Rev 11:11–12:

> Now after the three-and a-half days the breath of life from God entered them, and they stood on their feet, and great fear fell on those who saw them. And they heard a loud voice from heaven saying to them, "Come up here." And they ascended to heaven in a cloud, and their enemies saw them.

This describes God calling up the two witnesses, representing the Old and New Testament saints, up to himself in heaven. God does so because he is about to judge the unbelieving world. This event happens after the three and a half days have transpired, representing the time period between the time of Christ and the last judgment. Revelation 11:15–18 describes the seventh trumpet, which precedes the final judgment of God upon mankind. Because God is going to execute judgment, he calls his saints up to himself to be in safety.[8]

---

8. Beale with Campbell, *Revelation*, 230.

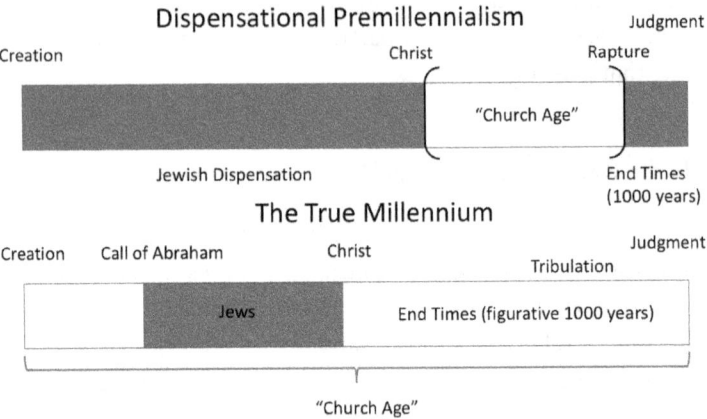

Figure 8. Comparison of the premillennial view of the thousand years and the biblical view of the millennium

As opposed to this, true biblical redemptive history in its entirety is equal to the church age (fig. 8). This is because God has had only one people all throughout history. God's program is saving lost sinners, whether they are in the Old or New Testament.

# Evangelical Errors Concerning *Sola Scriptura*

> For I have not shunned to declare to you the whole counsel of God.
> ACTS 20:27

## Introduction

FRANCIS SCHAEFFER SOUNDED THE alarm bells of compromise with biblical authority way back in the 1960s, 70s, and 80s. Even back then, an increasing number of churches and seminaries questioned the absolute authority of Scripture. This was a direct result of the secular impact of the world on the church. As a result, the church began to look to alternative authorities to augment the Bible. Schaeffer diagnosed Evangelicalism, that one of the main symptoms of this trend would be the divorce of facts from faith. In other words, the Bible is held to be true only when it talks about faith but not about its propositions.[1]

Back in the 1960s, Schaeffer described this trend in Evangelicalism as a watershed event. A watershed is a place on a mountainside where the water flows down on both sides. As the waters flow downward, they depart further and further away from one another.

Now in the 2020s, the situation is much, much worse, and the waters have divided from one another quite substantially. The question could be asked today, is the broader evangelical church still evangelical?

There are certain trends among Evangelicals that lead to a relaxing of the principle of *sola Scriptura*. Since this principle is so important for the

---

1. Schaeffer, *Great Evangelical Disaster*, 50.

discovery of biblical truth, it is important that we examine our own beliefs to see if we are somehow breaking or relaxing *sola Scriptura*. I have identified five areas where this is taking place within evangelical circles. These are the following: evangelical individualism, Arminian minimalism ecumenical cross-sectioning, biblical reductionism, and open theism.

### Evangelical Individualism

Evangelical individualism commits the error of ignoring the testimony of the Holy Spirit in the saints who have gone before us. Although the church is not an absolute authority, it is still useful to examine what other saints who have gone before us have thought about different issues. Interpreting the Bible does not happen in a vacuum all alone by oneself. Isn't it a blessing that others have gone before us and experienced certain things about God that they can pass on to us in latter days, even though they were imperfect?

This error manifests itself in such statements like "read the Bible as though you're reading it for the very first time." The individual cannot say that Christianity begins with them, and that they have a monopoly on the Holy Spirit. The Holy Spirit acts all throughout church history, since the beginning of the church. God acts through his people, as they pass on the gospel to others. God has saved a people for himself all throughout the world, but also all throughout *time*.

Furthermore, to always read the Bible as though you're reading it for the first time is to demolish any work that the Holy Spirit may have done in you in previous Bible studies.

Of course, antiquity does not automatically mean that someone is right. There is a saying in Hungarian: "More eyes see more things."[2] This means that if many believers are coming to the same conclusion regarding a certain issue, then it's a sign that that view might be correct.

### Arminian Minimalism

Another widespread error is what I would call Arminian minimalism. Arminianism believes that salvation is by grace plus choice, and Christ plus the believer making the choice; therefore it is an error. Jesus says that he chose us, and not the other way around (John 15:16). This leads to a skewed

---

2. Two heads are better than one.

method of evangelizing. Arminians will do anything to coax, cajole, or influence nonbelievers into "making a decision for Christ." As such, there is a tendency in many places to reduce the gospel into a minimal set of verses, a sort of minimal gospel, which Arminians think is necessary to tell a nonbeliever to understand and accept the gospel. Think of the Four Spiritual Laws, a sort of step-by-step procedure for guiding a person who has no knowledge of Christianity whatsoever to Christ.

Those of the seeker-friendly brand of Arminianism go so far as to block inconvenient verses from hitting the nonbeliever's ears in the fear that they will be scared off by these truths and will never accept the gospel. Theistic evolutionists in this manner will reinterpret the creation account in Genesis to fit in evolution and millions of years, so that nonbelievers will find it more palatable.

Seeker-friendly evangelization verges upon idolatry, since it makes the nonbeliever into a god who must be appeased. Imagine, what would happen if a nonbeliever came to Christ based on a minimal Arminian gospel? What if, after his conversion, he stumbles upon one of these hard-to-swallow sayings in the Bible? Will he reject those verses and expunge them from his Bible? This is humanism and doesn't speak well about such a person's standing before God. Would such a person even de-convert after discovering such hard to accept verses? Seeker-friendly evangelizing is very problematic.

The Bible tells us that the apostle Paul did not shun to declare to his hearers the whole counsel of God (Acts 20:27). Arminian minimalism and its brother, ecumenical cross-sectioning, both contradict the principle of *tota Scriptura*. These two errors state that man decides which truths are heard and which are relegated to a taboo status, never to be mentioned. Since they violate *tota Scriptura*, then by logical consequence, they also break *sola Scriptura* as well.

Arminianism also makes the error of common ground with the nonbeliever. Common ground means that there is a set of facts and evidence that both a believer and a nonbeliever can accept, which lead the unregenerate, non-believing person to faith in Christ. These facts are allegedly neutral, meaning that a nonbeliever, without the Holy Spirit, can understand them. Then, based on the nonbeliever's sovereign will, he will either accept or reject Christ.[3]

---

3. Jordan, *Failure of American Baptist*, 57–61.

Obviously, the Arminian will try to shield the nonbeliever from anything that would disrupt this process, even if it is an "offensive" Bible verse. Sadly, Arminians disregard Heb 4:12, which talks about the potency of the word of God:

> *The word of God is living and powerful*, and sharper than any two-edged sword, piercing even to the division of soul and spirit, and of joints and marrow, and is a discerner of the thoughts and intents of the heart.

Furthermore, according to Isa 55:10–11:

> For as the rain comes down, and the snow from heaven, and do not return there, but water the earth, and make it bring forth and bud, That it may give seed to the sower and bread to the eater, so shall My word be that goes forth from My mouth; *it shall not return to Me void, but it shall accomplish what I please, And it shall prosper in the thing for which I sent it.*

We also read Paul's exhortation to his disciple, Timothy, to preach the word at all times in 2 Tim 4:2: "Preach the word! Be ready *in season and out of season*. Convince, rebuke, exhort, with all longsuffering and teaching."

Jesus encourages his listeners to spread the word in the Sermon on the Mount in Matt 5:14–15:

> You are the light of the world. A city that is set on a hill cannot be hidden. Nor do they light a lamp *and put it under a basket*, but on a lampstand, and it gives light to all who are in the house.

## Is Free Will the Whole Picture?

Besides the previous issues, Arminian theology suffers another defect when it comes to *sola Scriptura*. This defect stems from its imbalance regarding divine immanence and transcendence. For an overview, see fig. 9. Arminian theology, with its remonstrant roots from the seventeenth century, overemphasize the human element in conversion. Arminians have a strong tendency to stress the need for the human response to the gospel, so much as to make it the decisive factor in conversion. No decision for Christ, no salvation.

# EVANGELICAL ERRORS CONCERNING SOLA SCRIPTURA

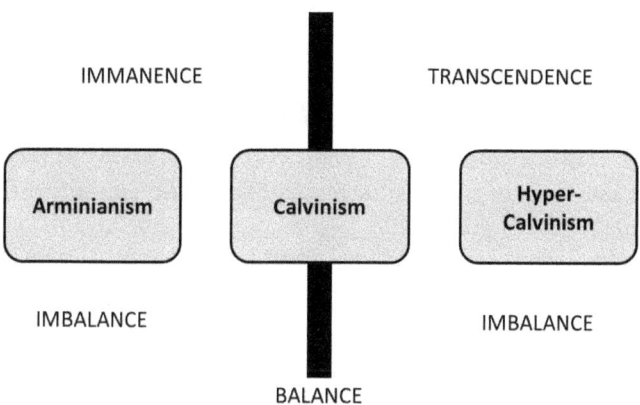

Figure 9. The Arminian view puts too much emphasis on God's immanence and is imbalanced, just as is hyper-Calvinism.

Arminians bring up such verses from the Bible that speak about repenting and exercising faith, such as when the apostle Peter exhorts his listeners to repent and be baptized for the remission of sins (Acts 2:38) or when we are told to trust in the Lord with all our heart (Prov 3:5).

This theological viewpoint is decidedly immanent, as opposed to what Arminians view as a totally transcendent view (what they incorrectly perceive as the Calvinist view), where God does literally all the work in salvation (by the Holy Spirit), and where prayer and evangelization are are almost unnecessary.

This viewpoint stresses such verses that emphasize God's sovereignty, such as how God works all things to the counsel of his will (Eph 1:11), or the fact that it is Jesus who chooses us and not the other way around (John 15:16).

In this, Arminians are correct. However, they mistakenly attribute this theological viewpoint to proper Calvinist theology. This viewpoint is only a caricature of Calvinism—it is properly known as hyper-Calvinism and is just as much of an imbalance as is Arminianism.

Both viewpoints (Arminian and hyper-Calvinist) present only half the picture! It is Calvinism that upholds both man's free will and God's sovereignty. According to Calvinism, man has the freedom to choose Jesus and follow him. The gospel invitation does go out to everyone, and it is incumbent upon man to have faith and trust in Christ for salvation. No informed Calvinist debates this.

However, Calvinism also teaches that God is sovereign, and that he alone gives faith as a gift. Faith is nothing man generates within himself. Without God giving faith, man cannot do much with his man-made faith. God does foreordain every single event that happens in the world (Ps 33:11; Eph 1:11). God does save some to be his people and passes by multitudes of other people. God foreordains the place, the manner, and the instruments in bringing someone to faith.

How do these two things go together? This was a puzzle that I tried to tease out for many years. I had to realize that man's will and God's sovereignty are in a mystical tension with one another. Both are true at the same time. This is different than Islamic fatalism since an element of divine mystery is involved. It is a mystery that man's finite mind cannot comprehend, just like the Trinity.

This is the Calvinist doctrine of concurrence.[4] Calvinism accepts those sets of Bible verses that speak of man's ability to choose Christ for salvation but also those that speak of God's sovereignly predetermining each event that happens in the universe—even our choices.

Besides those verses that speak of man's free will and God's sovereignty, there are also those verses that speak of both these things in the same breath. For example, Phil 2:12–13 says: "Therefore, my beloved, as you have always obeyed, not as in my presence only, but now much more in my absence, work out your own salvation with fear and trembling; for it is God who works in you both to will and to do for His good pleasure." In other words, man must work for his salvation, the reason being that God is the one who works in him both to will and to do. In v. 12 man is the subject of working out his salvation, but in v. 13 the subject switches to God who does these things.

Another example of concurrence is described in 2 Sam 24:1–10. Here God moves King David to number his people. David lends himself to this task, showing his pride as if he himself had built his own nation, not God. Verse 1 tells us that God moved David, yet when we reach v. 10, we read that David's heart condemned himself, because he had sinned greatly in what he had done. Yet another example is when Judas admits that he had sinned by betraying innocent blood (Matt 27:4), yet it was God's foreordained plan to sacrifice his own Son for our sins (Acts 2:22–24).

Arminian theology's inherent theological imbalance leads it to disregard those Bible verses that clearly speak of God's sovereignty. Even

---

4. Cserhati, *Critique of Provisionism*, 40–53.

though many Arminians claim to believe the doctrine of *sola Scriptura*, still, because of a prior commitment to theological immanence, they do not believe in *tota Scriptura*. If one Bible verse is true, so are all the rest. We must accept the entire testimony of the Scriptures, not those that support our prior theology. In this way Arminianism errs and in practice does not hold to *sola Scriptura*.

This trend is symptomatic of a broader phenomenon within Evangelicalism. Some Evangelicals tend to formulate a picture of what they think a loving God should be like. They don't like the idea of a sovereign God who decides salvation for us, bypassing the will of man. As such this is why some Arminian Evangelicals are negatively disposed towards God when the core of the problem is in their own (false) views of God.

### Ecumenical Cross-Sectioning

Many Evangelicals are active in the ecumenical movement. Sadly, with the involvement from the Roman Catholic Church, ecumenism should rightly be classified as a brand of syncretism. In other contexts, such as in foreign missions, it is practically unavoidable, with the involvement of multiple evangelical denominations trying to reach a people group together.

Ecumenical cross-sectioning is the practice of either watering down, reinterpreting, or ignoring certain Bible verses to avoid controversy and contention between believers of different viewpoints and denominations. People compromise for the sake of unity. What this means is focusing on viewpoints that all participants can agree on, in other words, finding a common denominator or a cross-section into which everyone can fit. The larger the number of participants and the more denominations are taking part, the smaller the cross-section. This is an inverse relationship.

On the foreign mission field, this can be a problem. For example, if believers differ on baptism, then in a multidenominational church plant, would babies be baptized?

When Rome comes onto the ecumenical scene, compromise is too great, since several elements of the gospel, for example, assurance and predestination and salvation by faith alone, will have to be left out so that Roman Catholics will not be offended. Rome condemns the biblical teaching of assurance and calls it the sin of presumption.[5]

---

5. The Council of Trent said: "If anyone says that a man who is born again and justified is bound *ex fide* to believe that he is certainly in the number of the predestined, let

As we can see, this is highly undesirable. At this point, not only are *tota Scriptura* and *sola Scriptura* violated, but the gospel is also compromised, which makes evangelization impossible. Thus, the modern ecumenical movement is in error, and compromising Evangelicals should withdraw and expend their efforts and energy elsewhere.

At this point it is better to offend with the gospel than to compromise it and possibly stand under condemnation by God.

## Biblical Reductionism

Biblical reductionism is when certain parts of the Bible are emphasized over against other parts of the Bible so much that these other parts are outright ignored. This leads to the phenomenon of "New Testament" only churches, which jettison the entire Old Testament. Other versions of this error claim that the gospel alone, or even just the Beatitudes only, are inspired by God.[6] This stems from a denial of *tota Scriptura*, and with it, *sola Scriptura*.

## Open Theism

Open theism is a newly developed heretical interpretation of Scripture, God's nature, and salvation, all bound into one.[7] This view really demonstrates how a false view of the authority and sufficiency of God's word ultimately leads to a false view of God himself, while distorting salvation as well. Because of its distortions, it can in no way be called Christian.

Open theism approaches the question of salvation in a *truly consistent Arminian way*. During the Middle Ages the Protestant Reformation emphasized God's sovereignty in salvation in opposition to the Roman Catholic Church. Rome taught a works-based salvation, whereas Luther, Calvin, and the Reformers stressed salvation by Christ alone, by grace alone, and by faith alone. With the advent of Arminianism, God's sovereignty is again being called into question by overemphasizing man's autonomous, libertarian free will as opposed to God's election.

---

him be anathema" (canon 15, in Schroeder, *Canons and Decrees*, 44). "If anyone says that he will for certain, with an absolute and infallible certainty, have that great gift of perseverance even to the end, unless he shall have learned this by a special revelation, let him be anathema" (canon 16, in Schroeder, *Canons and Decrees*, 44).

6. Mueller, *Called to Believe*, 39.
7. Less than a century old.

William Hasker reasons thus: if God believes that a specific event concerning a certain person will come to pass in the future, then that event by necessity must come to pass. This is due to God's divine infallibility. Therefore, this event will come to pass, whether the person wills it or not.[8] The point of concern for the open theist is the bypassing of man's autonomous, libertarian free will. Therefore, the open theist works by reversing the logic, starting from the standpoint of man's will. If man has free will, then man also influences future events—in other words, the future is open. God himself learns about events as they transpire.[9] Rhoda et al. argue that "libertarian free agency holds that which choice a libertarian free agent makes is causally open until the choice is made."[10]

Libertarian free will entails that a moral agent is free, in that whatever choice he makes, he could have chosen differently. Man as a free moral agent retains the right to such free will choices. The problem that open theists have with what they call determinism is that if God knows what choice men make, then they are not free. As such, all future events and choices become unpredictable, even from God's perspective.[11]

All this means that God by logical necessity cannot know the future for certain. God only reacts to the present situation. Some authors say that God does not determine every last detail of every single event; rather he "manages" things. That is to say, if he manages things, that means *he leaves certain things open* either to chance or to his creatures. In fact, open theists go so far as stating that humans with their libertarian free will *are able to help God in creating the future.*[12]

Open theists accuse orthodox theology as being heavily influenced by Platonic theology, which holds to stasis and determinism, including the future, settled down to the last detail. Ironically, these self-same open theists are open to interpreting the Bible based on modern scientific ideas of quantum physics. According to the Heisenberg uncertainty principle, there is a limit to the precision of the position and the momentum of a given elementary particle. Thus, uncertainty is woven into the fabric of the universe, meaning that the future is truly open and unknown. Since all truth is God's truth—even scientific theories—then the Christian church must go

---

8. Hasker, "Foreknowledge and Necessity," 122–29.
9. Pinnock et al., *Openness of God*, 15–17.
10. Rhoda et al., "Open Theism, Omniscience," 436–37.
11. B. Ware, *God's Lesser Glory*, 34–36; Flowers, *Potter's Promise*, 42.
12. Boyd, *God of the Possible*, 91, 94.

with the flow and incorporate it into its interpretation of the Bible.[13] This same reasoning lies behind theistic evolution.

Greek philosophy is a very broad area, and there were many different schools of Greek philosophy all throughout the ages, sometimes competing with one another. One cannot simplistically pigeonhole all of Greek philosophy into one single uniform category. One such pair of competing Greek philosophies were the Stoics and the Epicureans. At a basic level, the Stoics believed that natural laws controlled all events, whereas the Epicureans believed in the possibility of random chance, of indeterminism. For example, Epicurus writes to his friend, Menoeceus: "Necessity destroys responsibility and chance is inconstant; whereas our own actions are autonomous, and it is to them that praise and blame naturally attach."[14] Here Epicurus sounds much like an open theist!

The main issue is this: if man truly has free will to accept Christ's atoning death on his behalf, then ultimately, no one knows what the final makeup of the population of heaven will be like in eternity. As such there are things that even God does not know, because it is not God's decision as to who gets saved. Most Arminians will deny this, but they are doing so only because they are inconsistent.[15] Ultimately the human element determines God's choice of who gets saved and who doesn't.[16] Yet in John 15:16, we read: "You did not choose Me, but I chose you and appointed you that you should go and bear fruit."

What is further disturbing about open theism is if we consider that as Christians, we sin daily. Sin separates us from God. If God's sovereign election does not hold, we therefore cannot be certain whether we will be saved or not. How can we say we have an abiding relationship with Christ when we constantly drive him away with our sins? Open theism results in a constant state of changing back and forth between a saved and an unsaved state. In this manner it is ultimately man's work to change his status again and again to being saved. This results in a works-based view of salvation. In contrast, Calvinism assures the elect that they cannot ever lose their salvation.

But open theism goes even further. If God does not know who is saved, this means that God is also not omniscient. God's sovereignty and

---

13. Boyd, *God of the Possible*, 107–10.
14. Epicurus, "Letter to Menoeceus," para. 8.
15. T. Lewis, email to author, May 29, 2024.
16. Cserhati, *Critique of Provisionism*, 72–73.

his omniscience are closely connected to one another. Since God is also not omnipotent, this means that God is not God, and we therefore end up with nothing more than atheism!

The god of open theism, moreover, is finite. If God is neither omniscient nor omnipotent, he is neither omnipresent, immutable, impeccable, nor impassable.[17] Since God does not know the future, he must adapt to it; therefore he is subject to change. If he is not omnipresent, he exists in time, meaning that the god of open theism is a creature, rather than the Creator.

Contra Scripture, open theism claims that God does not know the future comprehensively. But this is precisely the position that the Bible takes. Because open theism presupposes a finite, ignorant god, it must therefore reject the testimony of the Scripture on God's omniscience.

For example, Ps 139 could be cited in its entirety, but let the first four verses suffice: "O Lord, You have searched me and known me. You know my sitting down and my rising up; you understand my thought afar off. You comprehend my path and my lying down, and are acquainted with all my ways. For there is not a word on my tongue, but behold, O Lord, You know it altogether" (Ps 139:1–4).

Jesus many times knew the thoughts of men. For example, he could discern the wicked thoughts of the scribes who called him a blasphemer (Matt 9:1–9). He also told Nathanael what location he was at (under a fig tree) before he came to him. Because of this, Nathanael praised Jesus as the Son of God and the King of Israel (John 1:43–49). God knows all things, because, by necessity, he has predetermined them: "In Him also we have obtained an inheritance, being predestined according to the purpose of Him who works all things according to the counsel of His will" (Eph 1:11). By his wisdom God created, founded, and established the world: "The Lord by wisdom founded the earth; by understanding He established the heavens; by His knowledge the depths were broken up, and clouds drop down the dew" (Prov 3:19–20).

Moreover, we could mention the numerous prophecies that God made through his prophets. In Isa 46:9–10, God says: "Remember the former things of old, for I am God, and there is no other; I am God, and there is none like Me, declaring the end from the beginning, and from ancient times things that are not yet done, saying, 'My counsel shall stand, and I will do all My pleasure.'"

---

17. Alpha & Omega Ministries, "Is the Future Settled."

Numbers 23:19 very clearly refutes the notion of open theism: "God is not a man, that He should lie, nor a son of man, that He should repent. Has He said, and will He not do? Or has He spoken, and will He not make it good?" See also 1 Sam 15:29. Isaiah 44:8 says that God declares the future from times long, long past: "Do not fear, nor be afraid; have I not told you from that time, and declared it? You are My witnesses. Is there a God besides Me? Indeed there is no other Rock; I know not one."

What is the remedy to open theism? We must realize that theological imbalances arise when there exists an imbalance between God's transcendence and his immanence. Transcendence is equated with God's sovereignty, that God is above all things and controls all events in history. In contrast, immanence means that God is close by, he is with you and interacts on a personal level. When transcendence is overemphasized, we get hyper-Calvinism. When too much stress is laid on God's immanence, we reach Arminianism.[18] The latter caricaturizes Calvinism as being so extreme to the point that it leaves out any interaction between the Creator and the creature. This is a straw man.[19]

While proponents of these two theologies are within the pale of Christianity, issues arise when God's immanence gets so much weight to the exclusion of God's transcendence. In open theism God so much becomes a part of this world that he loses all his transcendent characteristics, such as omniscience, omnipotence, and omnipresence, that he ceases to become God. Thus, a healthy balance of transcendence and immanence is necessary to complete the picture of who God is.[20] The Calvinist system does this well by emphasizing God's sovereign election and man's free will bound up in one.

---

18. Cserhati, *Critique of Provisionism*, 105–7.

19. Cserhati, *Critique of Provisionism*, 40.

20. B. Ware, *God's Lesser Glory*, 144–47.

# Conclusion

> If indeed you continue in the faith, grounded and steadfast, and are not moved away from the hope of the gospel which you heard, which was preached to every creature under heaven, of which I, Paul, became a minister.
>
> COL 1:23

## A Final Word

WE HAVE COME TO the end of this book, having surveyed a large number of alternative authorities and truth claims that come from places foreign to the Bible. We have also seen how scriptural authority is avoided, trampled over, or ignored in various ways. The enemy has many tools to try to trick the church into following falsehood. Jesus' words ring true: "And Jesus answered them, 'See that no one leads you astray. For many will come in my name, saying, "I am the Christ," and they will lead many astray'" (Matt 24:4–5).

We live in a day and age of great apostasy, and it is making inroads into the church. We need the church itself to be strong if we want to have an impact on the wider culture. First Peter 4:17 says: "For the time has come for judgment to begin at the house of God; and if it begins with us first, what will be the end of those who do not obey the gospel of God?" So many alternative authorities make bold truth claims and are vying for our minds. And this is why we must not be conformed to the world but be transformed by the renewing of our minds so that we may find the good, acceptable, and perfect will of God (Rom 12:2).

Scripture stands alone in all cases at all times. God doesn't need coaches or advisors. Let God be God, and let his word be his word.

Rightfully did Luther say that if we profess with the loudest voice every portion of God's truth, yet neglect to defend that one point that is under attack by the devil and his minions, then we are not truly confessing Christ. Where the battle rages, there must the soldier go, there lies the heart of the spiritual battle.[1]

As the church we must always hold to the exclusive, all-encompassing authority of Scripture. We must always "test the spirits to see whether they are from God, for *many false prophets* have gone out into the world" (1 John 4:1). We must reject all authorities and truth claims that originate outside the Bible, however persuasive and winsome they may seem. We must let the word of God rule our every thought and action.

Remember, the current era is very wicked, and the spirit of the modern age is opposed to Christianity and bent on its destruction. Its plan is to destroy biblical authority. As such, we must be exceptionally vigilant, for "if the foundations are destroyed, what can the righteous do?" (Ps 11:3).

As I wrote earlier in the book, as evangelical Christians, we need to know what *sola Scriptura* really means. We must also know how to articulate it, prove it, and defend it. Then, for those in the church who have been led astray, we must teach them and guide them to a better knowledge of the truth, all done in love. We must also pray for the truth of God to spread like a light in this dark world.

As part of this let us not forget to put on our spiritual armor, as described in Eph 6:10–20. Remember that all falsehoods, alternative truth claims, and perversions of the truth are lies of the devil, designed to deceive and lead people astray. Ephesians 6:14 describes the very first component of the Christian's defense, girding our waist with the truth. So many tragedies happen in people's lives because they have a false concept of God, and therefore believe a lie.

Let us always put our faith in God alone, in his word alone, and in the guidance of his Spirit alone.

**Heaven and earth will pass away, but My words will by no means pass away. (Matt 24:25)**

---

1. Schaeffer, *Great Evangelical Disaster*, 50–51.

# Bibliography

Adams, Jay E. *The Christian Counselor's Manual*. Grand Rapids: Baker, 1973.
Alexander, Desmond, T. *From Paradise to the Promised Land: An Introduction to the Pentateuch.* 3rd ed. Grand Rapids: Baker Academic, 2012.
Allen, Jason J., et al. *Sola: How the Five Solas Are Still Reforming the Church*. Chicago: Moody, 2017.
Allert, Craig D. *Early Christian Readings of Genesis One: Patristic Exegesis and Literal Interpretation*. Downers Grove, IL: InterVarsity, 2018.
Alpha & Omega Ministries. "Is the Future Settled or Open? James White vs Bob Enyart." YouTube, Aug. 10, 2014. https://www.youtube.com/watch?v=fxOOcJxEEYU.
Andrews, Edgar H. *The Spirit Has Come*. Durham, Eng.: Evangelical, 1982.
Aquinas, Thomas. *The Summa Theologiæ of St. Thomas Aquinas*. New Advent, 2017. Online ed. edited by Kevin Knight. Translated by Fathers of the English Dominican Province. https://www.newadvent.org/summa/.
Augustine. *On the Catechising of the Uninstructed*. In *The Nicene and Post-Nicene Fathers*, ser. 1, edited by Philip Schaff, 3:283–314. Repr., Grand Rapids: Eerdmans, 1980.
———. *On the Good of Widowhood*. In *The Nicene and Post-Nicene Fathers*, ser. 1, edited by Philip Schaff, 3:441–54. Repr., Grand Rapids: Eerdmans, 1980.
Bainton, Roland H. *Here I Stand: A Life of Martin Luther*. Nashville: Abingdon, 1950.
Beale, G. K., with David H. Campbell. *Revelation: A Shorter Commentary*. Grand Rapids: Eerdmans, 2015.
Bellinger, W. H., Jr. *Introducing Old Testament Theology: Creation, Covenant, and Prophecy in the Divine-Human Relationship*. Ada, MI: Baker Academic, 2022.
Boyd, Gregory A. *God of the Possible: A Biblical Introduction to the Open View of God*. Grand Rapids: Baker, 2000.
Buice, Josh. "Misunderstanding Cessationism." Delivered by Grace, Aug. 27, 2024. https://g3min.org/misunderstanding-cessationism-holy-spirit.
Burdick, Donald W. *Tongues: To Speak or Not to Speak; A Contemporary Analysis of Glossolalia*. Chicago: Moody, 1969.
Calvin, John. *Institutes of the Christian Religion*. Pápa, Hung.: Hungarian Reformed Church, 1909.
Clendenin, Daniel B. *Eastern Orthodox Christianity: A Western Perspective*. Grand Rapids: Baker, 1994.

# BIBLIOGRAPHY

Cloud, David W. *What Every Christian Should Know about Rock Music*. Port Huron, MI: Way of Life, 2016.
Crampton, W. Gary. *By Scripture Alone: The Sufficiency of Scripture*. Unicoi, TN: Trinity Foundation, 2002.
Cserhati, Matthew. *Atheism Unraveled: Powerful Proofs for the Existence of God*. Grand Rapids: Credo, 2016.
———. *A Critique of Provisionism: A Response to Leighton Flowers's "The Potter's Promise."* Eugene, OR: Wipf & Stock, 2024.
———. *Refuting Rome*. Omaha, NE: CreateSpace, 2017.
Dabney, Robert L. *Evangelical Eloquence: A Course of Lectures on Preaching*. Carlisle, PA: Banner of Truth Trust, 1999.
De Sales, Francis. *The Catholic Controversy: A Defense of the Faith*. Repr., Charlotte, NC: TAN, 2011.
Descartes, René. *Discourse on the Method of Rightly Conducting the Reason, and Seeking Truth in the Sciences*. Gutenberg, June 28, 1995; last updated May 13, 2022. Translated by John Veitch. https://www.gutenberg.org/files/59/59-h/59-h.htm.
Dodd, Charles Harold. *The Authority of the Bible*. Glasgow: Fount, 1960.
Ellicott, Charles John, ed. "Romans 16." Bible Hub, 1905. From *A Bible Commentary for English Readers*. https://biblehub.com/commentaries/ellicott/romans/16.htm.
Epicurus. "Letter to Menoeceus." Classics, n.d. Translated by Robert Drew Hicks. https://classics.mit.edu/Epicurus/menoec.html.
Eusebius. *The History of the Church*. Translated by G. A. Williamson. Middlesex, Eng.: Penguin, 1965.
Flowers, Leighton. *The Potter's Promise: A Biblical Defense of Traditional Soteriology*. Dallas: Trinity Academic Press, 2017.
Frassetto, Michael. *The Great Medieval Heretics: Five Centuries of Religious Dissent*. New York: BlueBridge, 2008.
Geisler, Norman L., ed. *Inerrancy*. Grand Rapids: Zondervan Academic, 1980.
Geisler, Norman L., and William C. Roach. *Defending Inerrancy: Affirming the Accuracy of Scripture for a New Generation*. Grand Rapids: Baker, 2011.
Geisler, Norman L., and Abdul Saleeb. *Answering Islam: The Crescent in Light of the Cross*. 2nd ed. Grand Rapids: Baker, 2002.
Gerstner, John H. *Wrongly Dividing the Word of Truth: A Critique of Dispensationalism*. Draper, VA: Apologetics, 2009.
Giberson, Karl W. *Saving Darwin: How to Be a Christian and Believe in Evolution*. New York: HarperOne, 2008.
González, Justo L. *The Early Church to the Dawn of the Reformation*. Vol. 1 of *The Story of Christianity*. Rev. ed. New York: HarperOne, 2010.
Greaves, Richard L. *Theology and Revolution in the Scottish Reformation*. Grand Rapids: Christian University Press, 1980.
Grenz, Stanley J., and Roger E. Olson. *20th-Century Theology: God and the World in a Transitional Age*. Downers Grove, IL: InterVarsity, 1992.
Harris, Samuel. *Letter to a Christian Nation*. New York: Random House, 2006.
Hasker, William. "Foreknowledge and Necessity." *Faith and Philosophy* 2 (1985) 121–57.
Hoekema, Anthony A. *The Four Major Cults*. Grand Rapids: Eerdmans, 1963.
Holmes, Michael W., ed. *The Apostolic Fathers*. Grand Rapids: Baker, 1989.
Hopko, Thomas. *Doctrine and Scripture*. Vol. 1 of *The Orthodox Faith*. Yonkers, NY: St. Vladimir Seminary Press, 1981.

## BIBLIOGRAPHY

Interdicasterial Commission. *Catechism of the Catholic Church.* Translated by the United States Conference of Catholic Bishops. Vatican City: Libreria Editrice Vaticana, 1993.

International Council on Biblical Inerrancy. "The Chicago Statement on Biblical Inerrancy." Dallas Theological Seminary, 1978. https://library.dts.edu/Pages/TL/Special/ICBI_1.pdf.

———. "The Chicago Statement on Biblical Inerrancy." *JETS* 21 (1978) 289–96.

Ioannidis, John P. "Why Most Published Research Findings Are False." *PLoS Medicine* 2 (2005) 696–701.

Johnson, Dru. *What Hath Darwin to Do with Scripture? Comparing the Conceptual Worlds of the Bible and Evolution.* Downers Grove, IL: IVP Academic, 2023.

Jordan, James B. *Creation in Six Days.* Moscow, ID: Canon, 1999.

———, ed. *The Failure of the American Baptist Culture.* Greenville, SC: Geneva Divinity School Press, 1982.

Kapic, Kelly M., and Bruce L. McCormack, eds. *Mapping Modern Theology: A Thematic and Historical Introduction.* Grand Rapids: Baker Academic, 2012.

Kelly, J. N. D. *Early Christian Doctrines.* Rev. ed. New York: HarperOne, 1978.

Kildahl, John P. *The Psychology of Speaking in Tongues.* London: Hoder and Stoughton, 1972.

Kistler, Donald, ed. *Sola Scriptura! The Protestant Position on the Bible.* Morgan, PA: Soli Deo Gloria, 1995.

Kittelson, James M. *Luther the Reformer: The Story of the Man and His Career.* Minneapolis: Augsburg, 1986.

Klingbiel, Gerald A. *The Genesis Creation Account and Its Reverberations in the Old Testament.* Berrien Springs, MI: Andrews University Press, 2015.

Knox, John. *Selected Writings of John Knox.* Edited by Kevin Reed. Dallas: Presbyterian Heritage, 1995.

Lawler, Philip F. *Lost Shepherd: How Pope Francis Is Misleading His Flock.* Washington, DC: Regnery Gateway, 2018.

Letham, Robert. *Through Western Eyes: Eastern Orthodoxy: A Reformed Perspective.* Fearn, Scot.: Christian Focus, 2007.

Loop, Katherin A. *Beyond Numbers: A Practical Guide to Teaching Math Biblically.* Fairfax, VA: Christian Perspective, 2005.

Machen, James G. *Christianity and Liberalism.* Grand Rapids: Eerdmans, 2009.

MacArthur, John. *The Charismatics: A Doctrinal Perspective.* Grand Rapids: Zondervan, 1978.

———. *Strange Fire: The Danger of Offending the Holy Spirit with Counterfeit Worship.* Nashville: Nelson, 2013.

Marsden, George M. *Fundamentalism and American Culture.* Oxford: Oxford University Press, 2006.

Marston, George W. *The Voice of Authority.* Phillipsburg, NJ: Presbyterian and Reformed, 1960.

Masters, Peter, and John C. Whitcomb. *The Charismatic Phenomenon.* London: Wakeman Trust, 1993.

Mathison, Keith A. *The Shape of Sola Scriptura.* Moscow, ID: Canon, 2001.

McGoldrick, James E. *Heirs of the Reformation: A Study in Baptist Origins.* Cape Coral, FL: Founders, 2000.

Mohler, Albert. "Something Rotten in Denmark: Atheism in the Pulpit." Albert Mohler, Sept. 17, 2003. https://albertmohler.com/2003/09/17/something-rotten-in-denmark-atheism-in-the-pulpit/.

Mueller, Steven P., ed. *Called to Believe, Teach, and Confess: An Introduction to Doctrinal Theology*. Called by the Gospel. Eugene, OR: Wipf and Stock, 2005.

Osman, Jim. *Selling the Stairway to Heaven—Critiquing the Claims of the Heaven Tourists*. Kootenai, ID: Kootenai Community Church Publishing, 2015.

Packer, James I. *Fundamentalism and the Word of God*. Grand Rapids: Eerdmans, 1966.

Peters, Joel. *Scripture Alone? 21 Reasons to Reject "Sola Scriptura."* Rockford, IL: TAN, 1999.

Pinnock, Clark H., et al. *The Openness of God: A Biblical Challenge to the Traditional Understanding of God*. Downers Grove, IL: IVP Academic, 1994.

Pratt, Richard L., Jr. *Every Thought Captive*. Phillipsburg, NJ: Presbyterian and Reformed, 1979.

Qureshi, Nabeel. *No God but One: Allah or Jesus? A Former Muslim Investigates the Evidence for Islam and Christianity*. Grand Rapids: Zondervan, 2016.

Ramm, Bernard. *The Christian View of Science and Scripture*. Grand Rapids: Eerdmans, 1954.

Reed, Kevin. *Making Shipwreck of the Faith: Evangelicals and Roman Catholics Together*. Dallas: Protestant Heritage, 1995.

Rhoda, Alan R., et al. "Open Theism, Omniscience, and the Nature of the Future." *Faith and Philosophy* 23 (2006) 432–59.

Riddlebarger, Kim. *A Case for Amillennialism: Understanding the End Times*. Grand Rapids: Baker, 2013.

Robertson, O. Palmer. *The Christ of the Covenants*. Phillipsburg, NJ: Presbyterian and Reformed, 1980.

———. *The Final Word: A Biblical Response to the Case for Tongues and Prophecy Today*. Carlisle, PA: Banner of Truth Trust, 1993.

Ryrie, Charles C. *Dispensationalism*. Chicago: Moody Bible Institute Press, 2007.

Sahakian, William S. *History of Philosophy: From the Earliest Times to the Present*. New York: Barnes and Noble, 1968.

Schaeffer, Francis S. *The God Who Is There*. Downers Grove, IL: InterVarsity, 1998.

———. *The Great Evangelical Disaster*. Westchester, IL: Crossway, 1984.

Schroeder, H. J. *Canons and Decrees of the Council of Trent*. Gastonia, NC: TAN, 2009.

Sebesta, Robert W. *Concepts of Programming Languages*. 12th ed. New York: Pearson Education, 2019.

Smith, Brian. "Heaven Is for Real, but the Book and Movie Aren't." Verse by Verse Ministry, Apr. 28, 2014. https://versebyverseministry.org/bible-answers/heaven-is-for-real-but-the-book-movie-are-not.

Smith, Greg. "UCC Membership Decline: 2,193,593 to 773,539 (#1974)." So What Faith, Feb. 20, 2022. https://sowhatfaith.com/2022/02/20/ucc-membership-decline-from-2193593-to-773539/.

Smith, Morton H. *Harmony of the Westminster Confession and Catechisms*. White Hall, WV: Tolle Lege, 2010.

Strimple, Robert B. *The Modern Search for the Real Jesus*. Phillipsburg, NJ: Presbyterian & Reformed, 1995.

Tay, Joel. "Misrepresenting Creationism." *Journal of Creation* 37 (2023) 40–44.

# BIBLIOGRAPHY

Truly. "Snake-Handling Pastor Bitten by Deadly Rattlesnake (My Life Inside: The Snake Church)." YouTube, Aug. 16, 2018. https://www.youtube.com/watch?v=7OcoUyXiuUo.

Van Til, Cornelius. *Christian Apologetics*. Phillipsburg, NJ: Presbyterian and Reformed, 1976.

Venema, Dennis R., and Scot McKnight. *Adam and the Genome: Reading Scripture after Genetic Science*. Grand Rapids: Brazos, 2017.

Ware, Bruce A. *God's Lesser Glory: The Diminished God of Open Theism*. Wheaton, IL: Crossway, 2000.

Ware, Kallistos. *The Orthodox Way*. Rev. ed. Crestwood, NY: St. Vladimir's Seminary Press, 1979.

Whitaker, William. *A Disputation on Holy Scripture*. Cambridge, Eng.: Parker Society, 1849.

White, James R. *Scripture Alone: Exploring the Bible's Accuracy, Authority, and Authenticity*. Minneapolis: Bethany, 2004.

———. *What Every Christian Needs to Know about the Qur'an*. Minneapolis: Bethany, 2013.

Whiteford, John. *Sola Scriptura: An Orthodox Analysis of the Cornerstone of Reformation Theology*. Chesterton, IN: Ancient Faith, 1996.

Wiese, Bill. "23 Minutes in Hell: Bill Wiese." YouTube, Apr. 22, 2024. Posted by Way World Outreach. https://www.youtube.com/watch?v=Io-_vNFKN5Y.

Williams, Daniel Harrison. *Evangelicals and Tradition*. Grand Rapids: Baker Academic, 2005.

Woodbridge, John D. *Biblical Authority: Infallibility and Inerrancy in the Christian Tradition*. Grand Rapids: Zondervan, 1982.

Zauzmer, J. "Clergy Gather to Bless One of the Only U.S. Clinics Performing Late-Term Abortions." *Washington Post*, Jan. 29, 2018.

# Subject Index

Aaron, 30
Abelard, 105
Abihu (son of Aaron), 30
Abinadab, 15
abortion clinics, female pastors blessing, 92–93
Abraham, 41
absolute truth, of God's word, 2
"activating grace," harnessing, 37
Acts (book of), as a descriptive history, 51
Adam, 2, 27, 47, 84, 112, 129
Adventist Church, opposed to *sola Scriptura*, 3
*Against the Heresy of One Noetus* (Hippolytus), 10
Ahio, 15
Andronicus, among the apostles, 68
angel, told Mary not to be afraid, 38
angel of light, devil coming as, 42
angelic tongues, reality of, 59
Anglican Church, claiming apostolic succession, 124
animal sacrifice, going back to, 67
anti-authoritarianism, Western, 26
antinomians, stressing a set of verses, 103
apocryphal books, listing of, 113
apophatic theology, 121
apostasy, living in a day and age of great, 147
apostles
    existence of today, 66–69, 73
    performed miracles in the book of Acts, 52
    spoken word of their preaching, 94
    teaching by, 9, 52
Apostles' Creed, 8, 27
apostolic authority, of Paul, 104
Apostolic Brethren, Fra Dolcino a member of, 116
Aquinas, Thomas (1225-74), 12
ark of the covenant, transporting, 15
Arminian, shielding nonbelievers, 138
Arminian Evangelicals, 141
Arminian minimalism, 136, 137
Arminian theology, 138, 140–41
Arminianism, 46n12, 136, 137, 139
Assyrians, sent by God, 53
Athanasius (AD 296-373), 11, 113
atheism, 37
atheists, 88, 127
Augustine (AD 354-430), 11, 55
authorities, hierarchy of, 24–25
authority, 18, 24, 40, 121–25. *See also* church authority

Babel, God divided the languages of mankind, 58
Babylonian mythology, 90
"backstage entrance God," seeking, 42
baptism, believers differing on, 141
baraminology, 89, 89n34
barber, visions of, 60, 62–63
Barnabas, Jews of Berea and, 104

## SUBJECT INDEX

Barth, Karl, 78, 81–82, 92
Barthian liberalism, of charismatics, 70
Baruch, as a later addition to Jeremiah, 114
Basil of Caesarea, 120
believers, 73, 74, 124, 136
Bellinger, W. H., 87
Bereans, accepted Paul's teachings, 43
Berkeley, George, 37
Berkouwer, G. C., 81
Bible. *See also* Scripture
    adding to God's word in, 49
    assigning to the ancient Near East, 84
    built upon the foundation of apostles and prophets, 15
    defining a particular book as part of, 113
    detoured to read into it anything, 81
    as enough, 22, 49, 65–66
    every verse having the same authority, 31n22
    exhorting the church to watch out for wolves, 4
    on God creating everything, 24
    inerrancy and infallibility of, 20–22
    as the infallible divine source of revelation, 100
    infallible knowledge in, 62
    interpreting based on quantum physics, 143
    as a long sequence of Hebrew and Greek letters, 128
    needing an external interpreter, 110
    no longer the sole highest authority, 128
    not depending on human intelligence, 15
    not needing to be verified, 97
    as the only source of religious authority, 108
    as perfect, 112
    providing horizons and vistas for scientists, 84
    reading of, 81, 111, 136
    removed from the public sphere, 1
    as self-authenticating, 95
    signs and miracles quite rare in, 44
    as the sole highest divine authority, 17–18
    as the sole objective form of religious truth, 42
    as the sole ultimate basis for theology for Luther, 14
    as the source of all true doctrines for Wycliffe, 13
    as a unique book, 5
    validation of, 43
    variations in the text of, 111
    will of God in, 49
    written for us, not to us, 57
Bible verses, 31, 95–96, 125, 137, 139, 141
biblical inerrancy, liberals jettisoning, 118
biblical reductionism, breaking or relaxing *sola Scriptura*, 142
"biblical" theology, 91–92, 93
biblical tongues, have ceased, 51
Biden, Joseph, 2
BioLogos, theistic evolutionist organization, 84
bishop
    as the husband of one wife, 70, 103
    meaning the same thing as elder or presbyter, 39
Bock, Darrell, 20
bodily resurrection, of Jesus Christ, 127
Bogomils, 115–16
*Book of Discipline*, Scottish, 16
Book of Mormon, as an added book, 3
breastplate of righteousness, large birds defeating, 62
Brunner, Emil, 81
Bultmann, Rudolf, 78
Burpo, Colton, 63

cafeteria Catholics, as a faction, 101
Cardinal Cajetan, 14, 113
Calvin, John (1509-64), 14–16, 96, 142
Calvinism, 139, 140, 144, 146
canon, 52, 79, 80
canonization, from a Roman Catholic viewpoint, 25
*Catechism of the Catholic Church*, 94–95
catechisms, 26, 27
Cathars, 115–16

156

# SUBJECT INDEX

"catholic," meaning wholeness, entirety, or according to the whole, 27
catholic church, 27, 27n12
Cerularius, Michael, 120
cessationist view, of the gifts of the Spirit, 57
Cevenol priests, prophesy and, 56
charismatic, defining the meaning of, 74
charismatic churches, 38, 40, 69–74
charismatic movement, 36–75
    adding extra-biblical sources of revelation, 41
    appealing to vibrant emotionalism, 118
    central problem of, 39–44
    claiming that several groups practiced prophesy, 56
    contradicting the Bible, 72–74
    denying *sola Scriptura*, 117
    enthusiastic experience of God's love, 37
    false epistemology of, 48
    hyper-spiritualizing religion, 3
    individual atomistic church bodies, or "ecclesioles," 40
    on Jesus going to hell after he died, 72
    lack of formalism and experientialism, 118
    lacking a well-defined theology, 17n1
    leading away from the house of Scripture, 75
    members worldwide, 36
    missing the real meaning of Pentecost, 58
    moving past the Scriptures, 38
    not following *sola Scriptura*, 70
    on rational, logical thinking about God's word, 45
    ritualistic altar calls and repetitious praying in tongues, 119
    of the Roman Catholic Church, 46n12
    sharing traits with the Roman Catholic Church and liberalism, 75
    theological framework of, 74–75
    as trichotomist, 45
charismatic pastors, continuing snake handling, 71
charismatic Roman catholics, 118
charismatic theology, rejecting, 74
charismatics
    accusing evangelical Christians of rationalism, 36
    asking about supernatural experiences, 64
    on the Bible as the living word of God, 70
    bitten handling snakes, 71
    contradicting themselves, 63
    controlling when the Holy Spirit speaks, 73
    conversion stories of, 37
    demands for a local monopoly on the Holy Spirit, 118
    don't do anything without "asking God," 49–50
    encouraging each other to bear testimony, 38
    as a faction, 101
    following such men as Bob Jones, 67
    on human understanding as roadblock to the Holy Spirit, 53
    not truly capable of discerning the Spirit, 80
    reading from the Bible, 69
    as trichotomists, 39
Christ. *See* Jesus Christ
"Christian atheism" movement, in the 1960s, 92
Christian doctrine, foundation of all, 20
Christian faith, 3, 40. *See also* faith
Christian freedom, 28–29, 50
*The Christian View of Science* (Ramm), 83
Christianity, introducing man-made ideas into, 1
Christians, 45, 63, 74, 127
Christ's atoning death for sin, as fundamental, 127
Chrysostom, John, 11, 55, 122
the church
    existed all throughout time, 27
    foundation of already laid down, 67
    inheriting the heavens, 126

## SUBJECT INDEX

the church *(continued)*
    jettisoning bits and pieces of the Bible, 2
    leadership of as exclusively male, 69
    as a sideshow, 133
    tricking into following falsehood, 147
church age, 133, 134
church authority. *See also* authority
    Acts 17:10-11 and, 103–4
    as also of human origin, 97
    characteristic of the Roman Catholic Church, 18
    early theologians and, 100–103
church fathers, added symbolism to Genesis, 82
churches, elevating authority or traditions to a divine level, 18–19
Clement of Alexandria (ca. AD 150-ca. 215), 10, 55
clergy, interpreting the Bible, 112
common ground, error of, 137
concordance, 83, 90, 122
concurrence, Calvinist doctrine of, 140
congregation, *ekklesia* as the word for in Greek, 130
conscience, 16, 28
conservative Jesuits, as a faction, 101
conservativism, not equating with the Bible itself, 128
continuationism, 57
Coots, Cody, 71
Coots, Jamie, 71
corporate manner, God dealing with his church in, 53
corporate worship, importance of, 42
Council of Trent, 103, 109–10, 141n5
covenant, God making with his people, 6
creation, six days of, 77
creation myth, formulated in Babylon, 90
creation science, 85, 89
cults, 3, 7
custom, without truth as error, 11
Cyprian, bishop of Carthage (ca. AD 200-258), 10–11

Dabney, R. L., 80
Darby, John Nelson, 127
Darwin, 82, 105
Darwinian evolution, 77
King David, 15, 140
de Chardin, Pierre Teilhard, 88
de Sales, Francis, 106
deacons, as men and not women, 70
death, as a consequence of man's sin, 86
decisions
    making your own, 50
    as to who gets saved, 144
demiurge, of the Greek philosophers, 105
demons, 37, 63–64
demythologization, by Bultmann, 78
denominational tradition, Knox made room for, 16
denominations, 4, 27
Descartes, René, 2, 106
devil, 42, 64, 148. *See also* Satan
Didache (Greek for "teaching"), 8, 9
disappearance, of tongues, 54
dispensational premillennialism, 134
dispensational theologians, 128–29
dispensationalism, 126–34
    basic tenets of, 126
    detracting from the unity of the Scriptures, 129
    erring in its most elementary tenets, 128–29
    splitting up the Bible into different sections, 3
    teaching of *tota Scriptura* and *sola Scriptura*, 129
    tied to a Plymouth Brethren Bible teacher, 127
dispensationalists
    charismatic churches as, 50–51
    charismatics as, 61, 67
    dividing history, 133
divine infallibility, of God, 143
divine knowledge, trusting Jesus,' 22
divine revelation, man augmenting, 34
divine truths, understandings of changing, 87
doctrine of election, Christ choosing us, 62
Dodd, C. H., 87
dogma, in Eastern Orthodoxy, 123

## SUBJECT INDEX

Fra Dolcino, 116
Donatism, charismatic movement similar to, 46
"door of the sheep," Jesus as, 128
dreams, have ceased, 57

early Christians, on the gospel as memoirs of the apostles, 9
early church
    patriarchates of, 122
    returning to the spirituality of, 50
    *sola Scriptura* taught by, 8–11
early theologians, 54–55, 100
Eastern Orthodox Church
    as heir of the ancient (catholic) church, 121–22
    as a mix of mysticism, 120–25
    opposed to *sola Scriptura*, 3
    on the Protestant view as incorrect, 123n7
    on the supremacy of councils, 104
    treating Scripture as a part of tradition, 122
Ecclesiasticus, containing Protestant doctrines, 113–14
"ecclesioles," 40
Eck, Johann, 14
ecstatic tongues, occult groups speaking in, 57–58
ecumenical councils, held in cities in the east, 122
ecumenical cross-sectioning, breaking or relaxing *sola Scriptura*, 137, 141–42
ecumenism, 70, 117, 118, 142
Egyptian mythology, god Atum and, 90
El, as the supreme god of Canaanite mythology, 90
elders, as the husband of one wife, 70
empiricism, as a brand of humanism, 36–37
end-time prophecies, charismatic movement and, 37
Enns, Peter, 20, 81
enthusiasts, as a synonym for charismatic, 38

Enuma Elish, gods warring with each other, 90
Epicureans, 144
epistemology, discerning true and false, 17
Esther (book of), Roman Catholic version of, 72
eternity, knowing the final make-up of, 144
Eusebius of Caesarea, 56, 98, 99
evangelical Christians, on what *sola Scriptura* means, 148
evangelical church, false worship due to denial of *sola Scriptura*, 30
evangelical errors, concerning *sola Scriptura*, 135–46
evangelical individualism, breaking or relaxing *sola Scriptura*, 136
Evangelicalism, divorcing facts from faith, 135
Evangelicals, 81, 135–36, 141
evangelization, 29, 137
Eve (*Cheva*), 2, 27, 84, 112, 132
everlasting covenant of grace, between God and Abraham's descendants, 130
evolution, 1, 82, 86, 87
evolutionary materialism, 78
evolutionary theory, 18, 83, 86
ex cathedra, pope speaking, 107
exclusivity, of *sola Scriptura*, 32–34
experience, as only subjective, 40
extra-biblical revelation, 35, 60–65
extra-biblical traditions, in charismatic churches, 69–74
extra-biblical words, charismatics basing life decisions on, 39

faith. *See also* Christian faith
    Bible infallible on, 21
    contending for, 112
    contradicting the Bible, 72–73
    making reason the recipient of revealed light, 80
    not created by reason, 47
    as nothing man generates within himself, 140

faith *(continued)*
    putting in God alone, 148
    resting upon revelation to apostles and prophets, 12–13
    statements of, 26
The Faith Church, in Hungary, 38n5
faiths, all are equal, 2
false apostles, charismatic preachers as, 66
false prophecies, in the charismatic movement, 44
false prophets, 4, 40, 148
false statement, never coming from a true statement, 43
false teaching, as an alternative to the Bible, 4
false worship, pragmatism leading to, 29
falsehood, misinterpreting the Master's voice for, 81
female apostles, as a new idea, 69
feminist charismatics, on Junia as Paul's fellow prisoner, 68
Finney, Charles, 37, 38
Five Fundamentals, of the Presbyterian General Assembly, 127
flesh, not giving any chance to sin, 131
foreign mission field, differing on baptism, 141
forgiveness, types of, 101–2
fortress mentality, as a sign of a lack of faith, 22–23
Four Spiritual Laws, guiding a person to Christ, 137
Pope Francis, 101, 118
freedom, for the Christian, 28
Full Gospel Tabernacle in Jesus' Name, 71
Fuller Theological Seminary in California, 20
fundamentalist movements, 127, 132
future events, man influencing, 143

garden of Eden, first gospel (the protevangelion) preached to Adam and Eve, 27
Gemara, writings about the Mishnah, 33
Genesis
    account of creation, 91
    Johnson reinterpreting, 85
    as a myth, 83, 90
    as not the product of ancient Near East mythologies, 89–91
Genesis flood, Jesus mentioning, 22
gentile church, as members of the everlasting covenant, 130
Giberson, Karl W., 84
glossolalia. *See* speaking in tongues
gnostic movement, charismatic movement as, 41–42
Gnosticism, 10, 77, 83
God
    acting through his laws, 6
    created each animal according to its kind, 86
    created everything good, 90
    declaring the future from times long past, 146
    divided his word into two separate parts, 126
    establishing a single covenant with men, 129–31
    foreordaining every event in the world, 140
    knowing all things, 145
    learning about events as they transpire, 143
    making himself known, 43
    moved David, 140
    needing a spokesperson, the pope, 110
    neutral facts outside of, 91
    not knowing the future for certain, 143
    not serving mammon and, 83
    portraying in a degrading manner as idolatry, 30
    preserving his word from all error, 7
    revealing his infallible, inerrant word using sinful, fallible men, 7
    slew an animal to make clothes for Adam and Eve, 112
    sovereignty and omniscience as closely connected, 144–45
    using tongues uttered by a foreign people, 53

## SUBJECT INDEX

wishing to have a living relationship with us, 5
Word emanating from, 5
"God and me" mentality, living out, 26
godly Christian life, not happening by being "zapped" by the Holy Spirit, 48
God's image, man created in, 47
God's law, hedge around, 131–33
God's logic, compared to man's logic, 47
God's will, 6, 48–50
God's word. *See also* the Word (logos)
  authority and sufficiency of, 142
  book itself claiming to be, 113
  as enough to make the man of God complete, 91n38
  as infinite, 66
  Jesus identifying himself with, 70
  knowing, 43
  man's interpretation of, 97
  nature of, 5–7
  potency of, 138
  ruling every thought and action, 148
  sufficiency of, 22–23
  understanding, 78
golden calf, story of, 30
gospel, 87, 88, 137, 142
Great Tribulation, 38
Greek philosophies, 144
Gregory of Nazianzus, 120
Gregory of Nyssa, 121
Pope Gregory the Great, 113
Pope Gregory VII, 103
Grenz, Stanley, 20
Grosbøll, Thorkild, 92

Hadith, stories or oral traditions, 33–34
"half-Christian" denominations, 118
Harnack, Adolf von, 78
Harris, Sam, 92, 118–19
Hasker, William, 143
healings, 57, 73
heaven, description of, 65
Hebrews (book of), on God revealing himself to his people, 96
Heisenberg uncertainty principle, 143
hell, vision of landing in, 63

Henry the Monk (?-1148), 12, 115–16
Hensley, George W., 71
heretical movements, based doctrines on *sola Scriptura*, 115–16
hierarchy, of authorities, 24–25
Hippolytus (ca. AD 170-236), 10, 56
historical development, of *sola Scriptura*, 8–16
historical Jesus, not important to Bultmann, 78
historical miracles, of Jesus Christ as fundamental, 127
historical-critical method, employed by "biblical" theology, 91
*The History of the Church* (Eusebius), 98
Holy Scriptures. *See* Scripture
Holy Spirit
  acting all throughout church history, 136
  as the authority for the Eastern Church, 123
  the church having, 59
  de Sales on the illumination of, 106
  different levels of, 73
  evident in a godly person's life, 48
  gift of contradicting the Bible, 74
  ignoring the testimony of, 136
  illumination of, 47
  interceding for us, 60
  on Jesus at his baptism, 57
  making men understand his message, 107
  mistrust of, 106
  never bypassing the text of Scripture, 28
  as a person, 53
  putting all our trust in, 80
  residing only within charismatic circles, 45
  revealing truth in words and images, 123
  role of in the selection of the canon, 106
  speaking to individuals, 42
  speaking to people, 70
  speaking to us through the Scriptures, 28

## SUBJECT INDEX

Holy Spirit *(continued)*
    teaching all things and bringing to your remembrance all things, 55
    testimony of, 15, 106–7
    working among believers as a community, 26
human element, determining God's choice of, 144
human experience, 121, 124–25
human history, dividing, 96, 126
human mind, illuminated by the Holy Spirit, 48
human psyche, raising above that of Scripture, 77
human reason. *See* reason
human response, in conversion for Arminians, 138
human tradition, Scripture augmented by, 95
humanism, 33, 117, 137
humankind, as constantly evolving, 87
Cardinal Humbert of Silva Candida, 120
Hume, David, 37
Hus, Jan (1369-1415), 13
hyperbole, examples of, 59
hyper-Calvinism, 139

iconic imagery, in the Eastern Orthodox Church, 123
ideological currents, denying *sola Scriptura*, 117–19
ideologies, acceptance of false, 29
Ignaz von Dollinger, 104
*ijma* (the consensus of the community), 34
imitation, as not the same as following Christ, 57
immanence, meaning that God is close by, 146
incarnation of Christ, Barth's view of, 82
indulgences, as contrary to the Scriptures, 14
inerrancy, 7, 20–21
infallibility
    of the Bible, 127
    divine, 143
    as an exclusive characteristic of God, 105
    papal, 104, 105, 118
    scope of, 21
    of the Scriptures, 16
inheritance, being predestined, 145
*Institutes* (Calvin), 14–16, 96
Ioannidis, John, 85n26
Irenaeus (ca. AD 130-200), 10
irrationalism, 2
Irvingites, prophesy and, 56
Islam, scriptures and traditions, 33–34

Jansenists, prophesy and, 56
Jasher (book of), mentioned in the Bible, 114
Jehovah's Witnesses, 3
St. Jerome, on canonical books, 113
Jesus Christ
    as an Apostle and High Priest, 68
    on becoming as little children, 88
    chose us, 136, 139
    did and said many things not recorded in the Bible, 65
    died on the cross and his Spirit went up to the Father, 72
    driving him away with our sins, 144
    as an example and object of faith, 79
    as foundation of his church, 67
    on his and his Father's testimony, 110
    identified with his revelatory word, 55
    inseparable from his revelation, 7
    knew the thoughts of men, 145
    miracles of, 44, 45
    never prayed in tongues, 57
    only source of being saved, 46
    paralleling the word of God, 7
    placing under anathema, 103
    referred opponents to the Scriptures, 16
    revealing himself, 61, 112
    on scientific matters, 22
    Sermon on the Mount encouraging his listeners to spread the word, 138
    upbraiding the Pharisees, 32

# SUBJECT INDEX

verified his identity as the Son of God, 51
as the Word, the logos, 5, 49, 64, 96
Jews
   of Berea, 104
   as the church of the Old Testament, 131
   traditions of, 98
   will inherit the earth, 126
Jezebel, 4, 100
job, selecting, 49
John, as more useful than Jude in Eastern Orthodoxy, 123
Pope John XXII, declared apostolic poverty heretical, 116
Johnson, Dru, 85
Jones, Bob, 67
Judaism, 32
Judas, betraying innocent blood, 140
Judeo-Christian religion, *sola Scriptura* exclusive to, 32
judicial forgiveness, 101, 102, 103
Junia, 68, 69
the just, living by faith, 114–15
Justin Martyr, 55

Kaasa, Harris, 56–57
kabbalistic *Zohar*, 33
Kansas City prophets, 56
Kant, Immanuel, 77
Karaites (*Kara'im*), 32
kingdom of heaven, not everyone shall enter, 29
knowledge, 55, 88–89
Knox, John (1514-72), 16

languages, real, cognate spoken in Acts, 58
Latin Rite Catholics, as a faction, 101
law, keeping evil from getting in, 131–32
law of God, as the same as the will of God, 49
laws of logic, humans using before thinking, 44
Lazarus, died again after Jesus raised him from the dead, 45
Lazarus and the rich man
   rich man going to hell, 64
   story of, 41
lepers, only one out of ten returned to Jesus, 44
letters, forming sentences, chapters, and books, 128
Leviticus, focused on how to worship God, 30
LGBTQ ideology, support for, 2
liberal churches, accepting gay marriage and abortion, 92
liberal Jesuits, as a faction, 101
liberal morals, liberal theology coming with, 92
liberal pastors and theologians, some ending up as atheists, 92
liberal theologians, 87, 92
liberal theology
   demoting the word of God, 19
   end result of, 92–93
   playing by their opponent's rules, 119
   on recognizing the work of the Holy Spirit, 80
   using evolutionary theory, 87
liberalism
   as the archenemy of *sola Scriptura*, 78
   dissection and evisceration of the Bible by, 118
   erosive tide of, 76–93
   as inconsistent, 92
   infecting the modern evangelical church, 20
   interpreting Scripture based on reason and logic, 80
   multitudes of theological schools of, 76
   persisting in a different format, 93
   tendency to criticize some parts of the Bible, 32
   way of, 2–3
liberals, 92, 118
libertarian free will, 143
lies, of the devil, 148
lifeless liberalism, as the opponent of the charismatic movement, 50
linguists, on utterances produced by people speaking in tongues, 58

# SUBJECT INDEX

Linnaeus, Carl, 89
literal interpretation of the Bible, adherence to a strict, 127–28
living words, God's words as, 5–6
Locke, John, 37
logic, as a part of mathematical thinking, 43
Luther, Martin (1483-1546), 13–14, 16, 114, 142

magisterial usage, of God's word, 7
"Magisterium." *See* teaching authority of the church
mainstream denominations, spiritual lifelessness of, 50
man
    as a free moral agent, 143
    working for his salvation, 140
man with palsy, Jesus healed, 51
manifestation of the Spirit, given to each one for the profit of all, 53
man-made theories, of origin raising doubts, 84
man's will, in a mystical tension with God's sovereignty, 140
Mark (book of)
    ending verses of, 71–72
    summary of the instructions of Peter, 98
marriage, determining Mr. or Mrs. Right, 49
Mass, Rome withholding the cup from the laity, 103
mathematics, as not neutral, 21
Matthias, election of to the office of apostle, 68
Maximilla, prophetess, 56
McGowan, Andrew, 20
McKnight, Scot, 84, 85
McLaren, Brian, 20
Menoeceus, Epicurus writing to, 144
message of salvation, committed to writing, 95
*metanoia*, on a change of mind and heart, 47
Middle Ages, *sola Scriptura* in, 11–16
millennium, 128, 134

minds, clouded by sin misinterpreting Scripture, 27
ministerial usage, of God's word, 7
miracles, 44–45, 57
*Mirror of Simple Souls* (Porete), 116
Mishnah, writings formed on oral tradition, 33
mistrust of God, causing deviation from *sola Scriptura*, 35
modalism, 72
montanism, Holy Spirit tied to the believer, 117
Montanists, prophesy and, 56
Montanus, 46, 56
moral relativism, 79
Moses, 30, 51
Muslims' daily prayer, exact words of not found in the Qur'an, 34
mysticism, 118, 120–25
mythologies, of the ancient Near East, 90

Nadab (son of Aaron), 30
Nathanael, praised Jesus as the Son of God, 145
natural laws, described by mathematics, 43
natural theologians, grouped organisms together, 89
naturalistic Darwinism, advent of, 77
neoorthodoxy, created by Karl Barth, 81
neo-Protestant charismatic leaders, praying together with Pope Francis, 70
"neo-Protestant" churches, multitude of, 40
new Jerusalem, 67
New Testament
    everlasting covenant continuing into, 130
    God speaking only by his Son, 96
    quoting the seven books of the Apocrypha, 114
New Testament churches, including both Jewish and gentile believers, 131
New Testament only churches, ignoring the Old Testament, 129, 142
Noah, covenant of, 129–30

## SUBJECT INDEX

nonbeliever, making into a god, 137
nonbelievers, sharing the gospel with, 9
nonbelieving naturalist, scientific theory of a, 83
noncharismatic people, as "have-nots," 45

objective truth, Scriptures as the sole source of, 40
Old Catholic Church, 101, 105
Old Testament, 15, 96
*On the Catechising of the Uninstructed* (Augustine), 11
*On the Good of Widowhood* (Augustine), 11
Oneness Pentecostal movement, 72
open theism, *sola Scriptura* and, 142–46
opinion of man, as tainted, 100
oral tradition, 34, 98–99
Origen, 97, 99, 113
Orthodox Church. *See* Eastern Orthodox Church
Orthodox Judaism, 32, 33
out-of-body experiences, as visions, 63

Packer, J. I., 15
Palmer, Tony, 70
pantheism, of Egyptian mythology, 90
papal infallibility, 104, 105, 118
papism, Holy Spirit tied to pope (supramontanism), 117
parables, 23, 41
pastors, 74
paternal forgiveness, 101, 102
patience, making a man perfect, 112
patriarchates, as autocephalous in nature, 122
patriarchs, as major ecclesiastical leaders, 122
Paul
  on all the apostles meeting Jesus Christ, 66
  bitten by a snake without harm, 71
  encounter with the Jews of Berea, 104
  forewarning the church that grievous wolves will enter, 100
  given a thorn in the flesh, 71
  handing down the same gospel he received from others, 9
  on holding traditions, 8
  not shunning to declare the whole counsel of God, 137
  on prophecy as superior to tongues, 52
  referred opponents to the Scriptures, 16
  taught by Christ for three years, 68
Pelagian, Finney as, 37
Pentateuch, first five books of the Bible, 41n9
Pentecost, 58, 61
Pentecost movement, 73
Pentecostals, 56, 81
Peter
  exhorting his listeners to repent and be baptized, 139
  as the first pope, 127
  oral tradition of, 98
  referred opponents to the Scriptures, 16
  as the rock, 99
  sinned by associating with the Jews at Antioch, 131
Peters, Joel, 108–9
Pharisees, 44, 110
philosophical trends, theological liberalism and, 76–77
Pinnock, Clark, 20, 81
Pope Pius IX, 104
Platonic theology, orthodox theology influenced by, 143
plenary inspiration, 31
Polycarp (AD 69-155), 10
Poor of Lyons, as a response to luxuries and avarice of clergy, 12
pope
  claiming to be infallible, 104, 105, 118
  exclusive communication to the Holy Spirit, 106–7
  guided by the Holy Spirit, 46n12
  as the patriarch of Rome, 122
  special insight into the knowledge of God, 105
Porete, Marguerite, 116

# SUBJECT INDEX

power, of God's word, 6
pragmatism, 29
premillennial view of the thousand years, 134
presumption, sin of, 141
*prima Scriptura*, redefining *sola Scriptura* as, 84
Priscilla, prophetess, 56
prophecy
   in the book of Joel, 61
   by both sons and daughters, 58
   cessation of, 57
   explaining and applying the Scriptures, 51
   of God made through his prophets, 145
   as greater than speaking with tongues, 52
   as the greatest gift of God, 73
prophets, applying God's law, 6–7
Protestant model, source(s) of revelation in, 96
Protestant Reformation, emphasized God's sovereignty in salvation, 142
Protestants, 109, 112–13
Psalms, on meditating on God's word, 47
psychological torments, of Luther, 115
psychologists, Christians seeking counseling from secular, 91n38
Ptolemy, 90–91
pure information, from God alone, 124
pure source of information, as self-authenticating, 96
Pyrrhonism, 106

*qiyas*, as application of analogical reasoning, 34
Quakers, 28–29
Qur'an, 33, 34, 125

rainbow, everlasting covenant and, 130
Ramm, Bernard, 83, 88
rapture, as anti-Gospel, 133
rational thinking faculties, sharing God's, 43
rational thought, charismatic movement and, 45
rationalism, 2, 80
reason. *See also* human reason
   revelation versus, 80
   separated from God's thinking in Pentecostal theologies, 48
   unenlightened as the sole highest authority, 77
   using in a faithful and faithless way, 47
Reformation, Roman Catholic apologists during, 106
Reformed religion, having the fullness of faith, 103
Reformers, 106, 142
repentance, 46–47
"replacement theology," 131
"Resolution Concerning the Authority of the Pope" (Luther), 14
revelation
   according to Rome, 94–98
   as complete, 52, 55, 67
   continuing today contradicting the Bible, 72
   in the Eastern Orthodox Church, 123
   extra-biblical not needed, 38
   other forms of, 18, 23
   versus reason, 80
Revelation (book of), 128
rich man, suffering in hell, 41
righteousness, of Christ covering our iniquities, 112
Ritschl, 78
ritualism, denying *sola Scriptura*, 117
rock, word of God as, 23
rock music, in evangelical churches, 30–31
Rogers, Jack Bartlett, 81
Roman Catholic authority, Peters on, 109
Roman Catholic Church
   authority of, 101
   charismatic movement resembling, 46n12
   claiming apostolic authority to explain Scripture, 95
   claiming apostolic succession, 124

## SUBJECT INDEX

claiming binding authority, 19
as a fundamentalist church, 127
having something similar to the *ijma* of Islam, 34
as highly fragmented, 41n8
interpretational system used by, 33
on interpreting the Bible, 118
lacking in the fullness of faith, 101
not found in the Bible, 99
with one billion adherents worldwide, 36
opposition to in the Middle Ages, 12
on *sola Scriptura*, 1, 3, 7
source(s) of revelation in, 96
varying factions within and outside, 101
Roman Catholic priests, anti-clerical sermons against, 116
Roman Catholicism
allowing other denominations to call themselves churches, 118
attacking *sola Scriptura*, 94
contradicting the Bible, 103
denying *sola Scriptura*, 117
doctrinizing tradition and church authority, 39
high church rituals pf, 118
Luther and Calvin tried to reform, 30
priestly caste of, 88
repetitious, vain rituals and lengthy prayers, 119
revelation according to, 94–98
supplementing God's Word, 94–107
Roman Catholics
adding tradition to the Scriptures, 95
Irvingites were, 56
mistaking *solo Scriptura* with that of *sola Scriptura*, 97–98
mysteries through spiritual experiences, 42
stressing one set of verses over against the other, 103
rule of faith, judging all things, 10n9

salvation, 86, 131, 140, 142
sanctification, 102
Satan. *See also* devil

excluding God from creating, 90
Schaeffer, Francis, 97, 135
schismatics, charismatic as, 46
Schleiermacher, Friedrich, 77
science, 84, 88–89
"scientific knowledge," negating *sola Scriptura*, 78
scientific theories, 20, 85
scientists, Christian laid the base of modern science, 89
*Scots' Confession*, upheld the doctrine of *sola Scriptura*, 16
scriptural authority, false views of, 23
scriptural inerrancy, Johnson denying, 85
Scripture. *See also* Bible; Holy Scriptures
authority of, 13, 18, 76, 135, 148
available to all, 40
as the biggest miracle of revelation, 62
denial of the sufficiency of, 22
different parts of cannot be just jettisoned, 31
differentiating from all other forms of authority, 18
differentiation within, 123
as enough, 61
given by inspiration of God, 22, 31, 55, 65, 125
as the highest source of divine knowledge, 97
informing about a right conception of God, 30
interpretation of in "the mind of the church," 122
leaving to chase after visions and dreams, 61
meaning "to me," 79
needing to keep coming back to, 66
not teaching that they are "all sufficient," 123
receiving divine revelation through, 95
relating to tradition, 8
removing certain verses from, 76
Rome claiming to have a high view of, 95

# SUBJECT INDEX

Scripture *(continued)*
   ruling over emotions and experiences, 41
   as the sole form of untainted divine revelation, 18
   standing alone by itself, 95
   as the word of God, 112
   written for us and not to us, 79
   as the written form of tradition, 98–99
*Scripture Alone? 21 Reasons to Reject Sola Scriptura* (Peters), 108
search for extraterrestrial intelligence (SETI) programs, 89
second blessing, contradicting the Bible, 74
Second Commandment, prohibiting depicting God in any form, 30
secular impact, of the world on the church, 135
Sedevacantists, as a faction, 101
self-authenticating authority, table of, 97
self-authenticating nature, of the Scripture, 15
self-control, Christian persons practicing, 132–33
self-denial, culminated in Christ's sacrifice, 87
seminaries, on doctrines of biblical infallibility and inerrancy, 20
*sensus fidei* ("sense of faith"), 34
seventh trumpet, preceding the final judgment of God, 133
Shakers, prophesy and, 56
sign, 44, 51–53
sin, 86–87, 103, 132, 144
sinful woman caught in adultery, 102
snake-handling churches, existence of, 70–71
*sola*, standing for "sole" or alone, 18
*sola ecclesia*, error of, 115
*sola fide* (faith alone), 19, 114
*sola gratia* (grace alone), 19
*sola Scriptura* (Scripture alone)
   applying to a catechism or a statement of faith, 28
   breakage from causing denominational diversity, 75
   comparison of ideological currents denying, 117–19
   defined, 17–19, 24, 108
   denial of, 46n12, 76, 93, 122
   determining the source with the highest authority, 25
   deviating from, 35
   dispensationalism contradicting, 129
   as the epistemology of the Christian religion, 17
   evangelical errors concerning, 135–46
   excluding the charismatic movement, 74
   exclusivity of, 32–34
   as the foundation of all Christian doctrine, 20
   freeing Luther from guilt and despair, 114
   historical development of, 8–16
   implying a denial of itself as a logical fallacy, 43
   incorrect meanings of, 24
   refutation of Roman Catholic arguments against, 108–16
   relation to the other four *Solas*, 19–20
   status today, 1–4
   worship and, 29–31
Solas, interrelating with one another, 19–20
*soli Deo gloria* (all glory to God), 19
*solo Scriptura*, 24, 109
*solus Christus* (Christ alone), 16, 19
sovereignty, of God, 140
Sparks, Kenton, 20
speaking in tongues
   alive today contradicting the Bible, 73
   for all, 57–60
   cessation of, 53–57
   as the least of all spiritual gifts, 52
   modern as a false phenomenon, 60
   as a sign, 51–53
   sparse throughout church history, 56
   speaking in, 50–51
   as very subjective, 57

# SUBJECT INDEX

speech, of God, 83
Spirit, cannot be bound by anyone, 106
Spirit of Christ, as different than the Holy Spirit, 74
Spirit of God, bearing witness by and with the Scriptures, 123n7
Spirit of truth, Holy Spirit as, 28
spiritual armor, putting on, 148
spiritual death, tied to physical death, 86
spiritual dryness, spawning the charismatic movement, 36
spiritual lifelessness, coming from a denial of *sola Scriptura*, 50
spiritual pride, of charismatics against other Christians, 46
spiritual testimonies, in a charismatic church service, 38
spiritual world, existing unseen to our physical eyes, 64
Stephen, on the law of God as delivered by angels, 62
Stoics, 144
stool of a single leg, as unstable, 95
subjective experientialism, of charismatics, 40
*Summa Theologiae* (Aquinas), 12–13
"A Symposium on Speaking in Tongues," 56
syncretism, ecumenism classified as a brand of, 141

Talmud, commentary on the Old Testament, 33
Tanakh [the Old Testament], searching thoroughly, 32
taxonomy, science of, 89
teaching authority of the church, divine revelation through, 95
teachings, 99, 105
Ten Commandments, 6
Tertullian (ca. AD 155–220), 10, 113
testimony, of the Holy Spirit, 106–7
theistic evolution
    akin to authority of the Roman Catholic Church, 83
    bowing before evolutionary theory, 3
    Calvin rejecting, 14
    reasoning lying behind, 144
    as a recent development, 82
    reinterpreting the book of Genesis, 77
    widespread in many evangelical churches, 91
theistic evolutionists, 86, 88, 137
theological liberalism, 76, 77, 79, 117
theology, becoming liberal, 2
thinking
    from the Bible, 26
    charismatics inconsistent in, 47
three-legged stool, sources of revelation forming, 95
Tillich, Paul, 92
times past, multiple channels of divine revelation existed, 96
Timothy, Paul's exhortation to, 138
Tobias, 114
tongues. *See* speaking in tongues
Tosefta, supplement to the Mishnah, 33
*tota Scriptura*, 31, 137, 141
tradition(s)
    of charismatic churches, 69–74
    exaltation of over God's word, 33
    as human in origin, 97
    kinds of, 98
    meaning something that is passed on, 9
    must rest on Scripture, 26
    not making anyone perfect, 111
    not putting man-made on par with Scripture, 27
    as not self-authenticating, 97
    receiving divine revelation through, 95
transcendence, 146
transcendent view, as the Calvinist view, 139
transubstantiation, Wycliffe rejected, 13
trichotomist model, man made up of body, soul, and spirit, 45
trichotomists, 39
Trinitarian, Word of God as, 5
Troeltsch, Ernst, 91
true doctrine, separating from false doctrine, 100
true millennium, 134
truth, 18, 35, 83

## SUBJECT INDEX

unbelievers, tongues are for a sign for, 51
uncertainty, woven into the fabric of the universe, 143
uniformitarianism, form of, 91
Union Theological Seminary, liberalism of, 127
United Church of Christ, declining membership of, 93
unity, people compromising for the sake of, 141
Uzzah, struck dead by the Lord, 15

Valdes of Lyons (ca. 1140-ca. 1205), 12, 116
van Til, Cornelius, 27
Vanhoozer, Kevin, 20
Vatical I council, on the infallibility of the pope, 104
Venema, Dennis, 84, 85
verbal inspiration. *See tota Scriptura*
verses. *See* Bible verses
Victor, bishop of Rome, 115
Vincent of Lérins (d. ca. AD 450), 11
virgin birth of Christ, as fundamental, 127
visions
    cessation of, 57
    God giving even today contradicting the Bible, 74
    of a man was caught up to the third heaven, 65
    not the way God communicates to men, 64
    validity of, 60–61
vowel forms, in charismatic utterances, 58

Waldenses, 115–16
watershed event, Evangelicalism as, 135
Webb, Robert, 20
Westminster Confession of Faith, 27–28
*What Hath Darwin to Do with Scripture* (Johnson), 85
White, Ellen G., 18
Wiese, Bill, 63
will of God. *See* God's will
wisdom, of God, 145
Wisdom (book of), containing Protestant doctrines, 113–14
witnesses, God calling up to heaven, 133
women
    in charismatic churches, 39
    of the charismatic movement, 69–70
    as pastors contradicting the Bible, 74
the Word (logos). *See also* God's word
    Jesus as, 5, 49, 55, 96
word of God. *See* God's word
"words," functioning as revelation in practice, 39
works, covenant of, 129
works-based righteousness, of Johnson, 85
works-based salvation, 142, 144
worship, 4, 26, 29–31
written word, God revealing himself via, 14
Wycliffe, John (1324?-84), 13, 115

Cardinal Zomenes, on the Apocrypha, 113

# Scripture Index

## Old Testament

### Genesis

|   | 1, 3, 18, 83, 84, 85, 86, 90 |
|---|---|
| 1 | 84 |
| 1:5 | 24 |
| 1:10–11 | 89 |
| 1–11 | 77, 87 |
| 1:21 | 89 |
| 1:24–25 | 86 |
| 1:26–28 | 24 |
| 1:28 | 21 |
| 1:31 | 90 |
| 2 | 84 |
| 2:3 | 86 |
| 2–3 | 87 |
| 2:16–17 | 86 |
| 3 | 112 |
| 3:1 | 132 |
| 3:2–3 | 132 |
| 3:14 | 90 |
| 3:15 | 27 |
| 3:19 | 86 |
| 9:16 | 130 |
| 15:6 | 102 |
| 17:7 | 130 |

### Exodus

| 20:13–15 | 49 |
|---|---|
| 32 | 30 |

### Leviticus

| 5:5 | 102 |
|---|---|
| 10:1–2 | 30 |
| 16:21 | 102 |

### Numbers

| 11:29 | 51 |
|---|---|
| 22:28–30 | 85 |
| 23:19 | 21, 146 |

### Deuteronomy

| 12:32 | 16 |
|---|---|

### Joshua

| 1:8 | 11 |
|---|---|
| 10:13 | 114 |

### Judges

| 6:37 | 96 |
|---|---|

# SCRIPTURE INDEX

## 1 Samuel

| | |
|---|---|
| 15:29 | 146 |

## 2 Samuel

| | |
|---|---|
| 1:18 | 114 |
| 6:1–7 | 15 |
| 6:6–7 | 95 |
| 22:2 | 23 |
| 24:1–10 | 140 |

## 1 Kings

| | |
|---|---|
| 13:9 | 40 |
| 13:9–24 | 40 |
| 13:18 | 40 |
| 13:24 | 40 |
| 19:12 | 48 |

## Esther

| | |
|---|---|
|  | 114 |
| 10 | 72 |

## Psalms

| | |
|---|---|
| 1:2 | 47 |
| 11:3 | 148 |
| 18:2 | 22 |
| 19:7–8 | 6 |
| 19:10 | 65 |
| 29:3–9 | 6 |
| 31:3 | 23 |
| 33:11 | 140 |
| 49:3 | 47 |
| 50:1 | 6 |
| 63:6 | 47 |
| 66:18 | 102 |
| 71:3 | 23 |
| 77:12 | 47 |
| 84:11 | 60 |
| 91:2 | 23 |
| 103:12 | 102 |
| 119:78 | 47 |
| 119:97 | 1 |
| 119:105 | 22 |
| 139 | 145 |
| 139:1–4 | 145 |
| 143:5 | 47 |
| 144:2 | 23 |

## Proverbs

| | |
|---|---|
| 3:5 | 139 |
| 3:19–20 | 145 |
| 14:12 | 41 |

## Ecclesiastes

| | |
|---|---|
|  | 123 |
| 1:9 | 93 |

## Isaiah

| | |
|---|---|
|  | 123 |
| 28:11–12 | 53 |
| 44:8 | 146 |
| 46:9–10 | 145 |
| 55:10–11 | 138 |

## Jeremiah

| | |
|---|---|
| 6:27 | 23 |
| 16:19 | 23 |

## Joel

| | |
|---|---|
| 2:28–29 | 61 |
| 2:29 | 61 |
| 2:32 | 61 |

## Habakkuk

| | |
|---|---|
| 2:4 | 114 |

## Malachi

| | |
|---|---|
| 2:16 | 63 |

# SCRIPTURE INDEX

## Deuterocanonical Books

### Wisdom

| | |
|---|---|
| 15:7 | 113 |

## New Testament

### Matthew

| | |
|---|---|
| | 86 |
| 3:16 | 57 |
| 5:14–15 | 138 |
| 5:18 | 76, 88 |
| 5:39–41 | 87 |
| 6:9 | 73 |
| 6:24 | 83 |
| 7:13 | 101 |
| 7:21–23 | 29 |
| 7:24–25 | 23 |
| 7:24–27 | 23 |
| 9:1–9 | 145 |
| 12:38–39 | 44 |
| 12:43–45 | 45 |
| 16:16–18 | 1, 67, 115 |
| 16:18 | 95, 99 |
| 16:18–19 | 13 |
| 16:25 | 87 |
| 18:2 | 88 |
| 18:18 | 99 |
| 24:4–5 | 147 |
| 24:23–26 | 44 |
| 24:25 | 148 |
| 24:35 | 22 |
| 24:36 | 22 |
| 24:37–39 | 22 |
| 26:27–28 | 103 |
| 27:4 | 140 |

### Mark

| | |
|---|---|
| | 98 |
| 2:1–12 | 51 |
| 2:5 | 51 |
| 2:11–12 | 51 |
| 7:8 | 32 |
| 7:9 | 94, 98 |

| | |
|---|---|
| 16 | 50 |
| 16:9–20 | 71, 72 |
| 16:17–20 | 70–71 |

### Luke

| | |
|---|---|
| | 86 |
| 1:30 | 38 |
| 11:2–4 | 102 |
| 16:16 | 66 |
| 16:19–31 | 41, 64 |
| 16:27–31 | 41 |
| 16:31 | 36 |
| 17:11–19 | 44 |
| 19:10 | 51 |
| 23:46 | 72 |
| 24:25–32 | 112 |
| 24:27 | 112 |

### John

| | |
|---|---|
| | 123 |
| 1:1 | 49, 55, 70 |
| 1:1–3 | 5 |
| 1:43–49 | 145 |
| 2:11 | 44 |
| 3:5 | 46 |
| 3:8 | 73, 106, 107 |
| 4:21 | 79 |
| 5 | 16 |
| 5:24 | 79 |
| 6:35 | 79 |
| 6:40 | 79 |
| 6:47 | 79 |
| 6:63 | 5, 70 |
| 7 | 16 |
| 7:38 | 79 |
| 8:11 | 102 |
| 8:12–16 | 110 |
| 10:7 | 128 |
| 10:16 | 131 |
| 10:27 | 43, 96 |
| 11:25 | 79 |
| 12:44 | 79 |
| 12:46 | 79 |
| 13:16 | 68 |
| 14:1 | 79 |

## John (continued)

| | |
|---|---|
| 14:6 | 46, 70, 131 |
| 14:11–12 | 79 |
| 14:12 | 45 |
| 14:16 | 74 |
| 14:26 | 55 |
| 15:16 | 62, 136, 139, 144 |
| 16:13 | 21, 27, 28, 61, 80, 91 |
| 16:33 | 74 |
| 17:17 | 17 |
| 20:30–31 | 65 |

## Acts

| | |
|---|---|
| | 51, 52, 73 |
| 1:15–21 | 68 |
| 1:20 | 68 |
| 1:21 | 68 |
| 1:22 | 68 |
| 1:23–26 | 68 |
| 2 | 50 |
| 2:3 | 73 |
| 2:5–12 | 58 |
| 2:8 | 73 |
| 2:9–11 | 58 |
| 2:17–18 | 58 |
| 2:22–24 | 140 |
| 2:33 | 61 |
| 2:38 | 139 |
| 3:25 | 126, 130 |
| 4:12 | 131 |
| 5:29 | 12 |
| 7:38 | 130, 131 |
| 7:53 | 62 |
| 8 | 50 |
| 9:3–18 | 68 |
| 9:20–25 | 68 |
| 10 | 50 |
| 10:15 | 132 |
| 10:38 | 57 |
| 17 | 16 |
| 17:5–8 | 104 |
| 17:10 | 103 |
| 17:10–11 | 8, 43, 103, 104, 124 |
| 17:11 | 103 |
| 19 | 50 |
| 20:17–28 | 39 |
| 20:27 | 135 |
| 20:29 | 4, 100 |
| 28:3–6 | 71 |

## Romans

| | |
|---|---|
| 1:17 | 114 |
| 1:18 | 5 |
| 2:11 | 131 |
| 3:1–2 | 131 |
| 3:4 | 100 |
| 3:24 | 102 |
| 5:1 | 102 |
| 5:1–2 | 102 |
| 8:9 | 74 |
| 8:26–27 | 60 |
| 8:38–39 | 63 |
| 12:1–2 | 26, 46, 80 |
| 12:2 | 120, 147 |
| 13:14 | 48 |
| 16:7 | 68 |
| 16:17 | 100 |

## 1 Corinthians

| | |
|---|---|
| 1:10 | 100 |
| 6:19 | 73, 74 |
| 12 | 55 |
| 12:3 | 59, 73 |
| 12:7 | 53 |
| 12:11–13 | 59 |
| 12–14 | 50 |
| 12:27–28 | 130 |
| 12:28 | 52 |
| 13:1 | 59 |
| 13:2 | 59 |
| 13:8 | 51, 54, 55, 60, 73 |
| 13:8–10 | 53, 54 |
| 13:9 | 54 |
| 13:13 | 73 |
| 14:1 | 52 |
| 14:1–5 | 52 |
| 14:2 | 52 |
| 14:3 | 52 |
| 14:4 | 52 |

## SCRIPTURE INDEX

| | |
|---|---|
| 14:5 | 52 |
| 14:13 | 52 |
| 14:14 | 52 |
| 14:15 | 52 |
| 14:16 | 52 |
| 14:22 | 51 |
| 14:27 | 73 |
| 14:29 | 51 |
| 15:1–4 | 9 |
| 15:3–8 | 66 |
| 15:7–8 | 73 |
| 15:8 | 66 |
| 15:37–39 | 86 |

### 2 Corinthians

| | |
|---|---|
| 11:14 | 42 |
| 12:1–4 | 64 |
| 12:7 | 71, 73 |

### Galatians

| | |
|---|---|
| 1:6–8 | 8 |
| 1:11–18 | 68 |
| 2:11–14 | 131 |
| 3:27 | 48 |
| 5:13 | 132 |

### Ephesians

| | |
|---|---|
| 1:4–5 | 103 |
| 1:11 | 139, 140, 145 |
| 2:19–20 | 67 |
| 2:20 | 15, 67 |
| 4:11 | 66 |
| 6:10–20 | 148 |
| 6:14 | 148 |

### Philippians

| | |
|---|---|
| 2:12–13 | 140 |

### Colossians

| | |
|---|---|
| 1:23 | 147 |
| 2:8–10 | 74 |

### 2 Thessalonians

| | |
|---|---|
| 2 | 98 |
| 2:15 | 8, 26, 98 |

### 1 Timothy

| | |
|---|---|
| 2:12 | 39, 69 |
| 3:2 | 39, 69, 70, 74, 103, 118 |
| 3:8 | 70 |
| 3:11 | 69, 70 |

### 2 Timothy

| | |
|---|---|
| 3:16 | 31, 97 |
| 3:16–17 | 55, 60, 65, 73, 76, 91n38, 111–12 |
| 3:17 | 49 |
| 3:26–27 | 22 |
| 4:2 | 138 |
| 4:3 | 7 |

### Titus

| | |
|---|---|
| 1:5–6 | 70 |

### Hebrews

| | |
|---|---|
| 1:1–2 | 64, 74, 96 |
| 3:1 | 68 |
| 4:12 | 138 |
| 10:4 | 102 |
| 12:23 | 102 |
| 13:8 | 50, 88, 130 |
| 13:17 | 24 |
| 13:20 | 130 |

### James

| | |
|---|---|
| 1:4 | 112 |
| 1:27 | 49 |
| 4:4 | 78, 118 |

## 1 Peter

| | |
|---|---|
| 1:16 | 114 |
| 4:17 | 147 |

## 2 Peter

| | |
|---|---|
| 1 | 16 |
| 1:6 | 132 |
| 3:15–16 | 124 |

## 1 John

| | |
|---|---|
| 1:3–9 | 102 |
| 1:7–9 | 102 |
| 1:9 | 102 |
| 4:1 | 148 |
| 19:9–10 | 102 |

## Jude

| | |
|---|---|
| | 123 |
| 1:3 | 72, 112 |

## Revelation

| | |
|---|---|
| | 37, 128 |
| 1:1 | 61 |
| 2:20 | 4, 100 |
| 3:7 | 56 |
| 4:6 | 128 |
| 11:11–12 | 133 |
| 11:15–18 | 133 |
| 20:11–15 | 102 |
| 20:14 | 64 |
| 21:9 | 63 |
| 21:12–14 | 67 |
| 22:18 | 49, 75 |
| 22:18–19 | 19 |
| 22:19 | 65 |

# Early Christian Writings

## Chrysostom, John

"Twenty-Ninth Homily on the First Epistle of Paul the Apostle to the Corinthians"

    55

## Eusebius

*The History of the Church*

| | |
|---|---|
| | 98, 99 |
| 64 | 98n3 |

# Greek and Roman Literature

## Epicurus

"Letter to Menoeceus"

| | |
|---|---|
| para. 8 | 144n14 |

www.ingramcontent.com/pod-product-compliance
Lightning Source LLC
Chambersburg PA
CBHW070922180426
43192CB00037B/1679